ORTHO'S All About
Deck & Patio
Upgrades

Meredith® Books
Des Moines, Iowa

Ortho® Books
An imprint of Meredith® Books

Ortho's All About Deck & Patio Upgrades
Editor: Larry Erickson
Art Director: Tom Wegner
Contributing Writers: Steve Cory, Martin Miller,
  Dave Toht
Copy Chief: Catherine Hamrick
Copy and Production Editor: Terri Fredrickson
Contributing Copy Editor: Steve Hallam
Technical Reviewer: Raymond L. Kast
Contributing Proofreaders: Kathy Eastman,
  Colleen Johnson, Margaret A. Smith
Indexer: Donald Glassman
Electronic Production Coordinator: Paula Forest
Editorial and Design Assistants: Kathleen Stevens,
  Karen Schirm
Production Director: Douglas M. Johnston
Book Production Managers: Pam Kvitne,
  Marjorie J. Schenkelberg

**Additional Editorial Contributions from
  Art Rep Services**
Director: Chip Nadeau
Designer: lk Design
Photo Editor: Nancy South
Illustrators: Shawn Wallace, John Teisberg, Dave Brandon

Meredith® Books
Editor in Chief: James D. Blume
Design Director: Matt Strelecki
Managing Editor: Gregory H. Kayko

Director, Sales & Marketing, Retail: Michael A. Peterson
Director, Sales & Marketing, Special Markets:
  Rita McMullen
Director, Sales & Marketing, Home & Garden Center
  Channel: Ray Wolf
Director, Operations: George A. Susral

Vice President, General Manager: Jamie L. Martin

Meredith Publishing Group
President, Publishing Group: Christopher M. Little
Vice President, Consumer Marketing & Development:
  Hal Oringer

Meredith Corporation
Chairman and Chief Executive Officer: William T. Kerr

Chairman of the Executive Committee: E.T. Meredith III

Photographers
(Photographers credited may retain copyright ©
  to the listed photographs.)
Karen Bussolini/Positive Images: 11 (BL)
Dick Canby/Positive Images: 11 (TR)
John Fulker: 4 (BL), 5 (TR), 6, 26-27
Shelley Hawes/Decisive Moment Photography: 8, 9, 18, 24,
  61 (BR), 65 (bottom), 79 (BL)
Margaret Hensel/Positive Images: 57 (TR)
Jerry Howard/Positive Images: 6, 7 (TR), 12, 44 (top), 57 (TL)
Craig Lovell: 5 (TL), 57 (bottom)
Robert Perron: 4 (BR), 5 (BR), 7 (RC), 42–43, 45 (top),
  45 (BR), 56 (BL)
Ann Reilly/Positive Images: 77 (BR), 78 (BR)
Rick Taylor: Cover
Deidra Walpole: 5 (CR, BL), 7 (BR), 10, 11 (BR), 56 (BR),
  81 (bottom)
Unicorn Stock: 67

Acknowledgements
Additional photography was provided by:
Malibu Outdoor Lighting: 80 (bottom)
Wolman Wood Care Products: 19, 66 (bottom)

All of us at Ortho® Books are dedicated to providing you
with the information and ideas you need to enhance your
home and garden. We welcome your comments and
suggestions about this book. Write to us at:
  Meredith Corporation
  Ortho Books
  1716 Locust St.
  Des Moines, IA 50309–3023

If you would like more information on other Ortho
products, call 800-225-2883 or visit us at www.ortho.com

Note to the Readers: Due to differing conditions, tools,
and individual skills, Meredith Corporation assumes no
responsibility for any damages, injuries suffered, or losses
incurred as a result of following the information published
in this book. Before beginning any project, review the
instructions carefully, and if any doubts or questions remain,
consult local experts or authorities. Because codes and
regulations vary greatly, you always should check with
authorities to ensure that your project complies with all
applicable local codes and regulations. Always read and
observe all of the safety precautions provided by
manufacturers of any tools, equipment, or supplies,
and follow all accepted safety procedures.

MATERIALS AND DESIGN

A patio or deck should be a place where family and friends enjoy the outdoors within easy reach of all the comforts of home. But that's not always possible. Some patios and decks are awkwardly shaped; some are small and unattractive. Others would be just perfect with one or two amenities, such as shade or lighting. Yours may be adequate, but what would it take to make a big difference?

If your outdoor living area isn't user-friendly, if it's not an inviting place for entertaining or relaxing, then this book is for you. You'll find plenty of ideas for improvements, along with helpful directions that will show you how to make them yourself.

In the first chapter, we outline some planning and design tips and what to look for when choosing materials. Later chapters walk you through improvements that will enhance the surface of your deck and change the look of your railings and stairs. You'll learn how shade structures, fences and walls, furniture and planters, even plumbing and electrical service, will add to your outdoor enjoyment.

This book is about enhancing structures that are in reasonably good condition. If your deck or patio is in serious disrepair, and you need to build a new one, you may want to consult specialized sources on outdoor construction.

Unlike interior remodeling projects, outdoor repairs and additions don't need to disrupt your life. You can work on a project over several weekends without upsetting the household.

But whether the job takes a lot of time— or only a little—be sure to read the instructions completely before you start. That way you'll get a realistic sense of how much time to budget for the job.

Transform obstacles into accents by incorporating them into your design. Don't let trees and other natural elements prevent you from changing your deck or patio. Here, the lightly stained and angled decking wraps around a large oak to enhance this outdoor retreat. Potted plants add a dash of color.

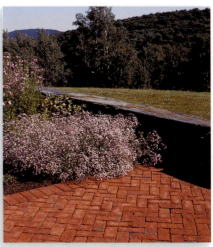

Need to define a boundary without destroying a favorite view? This low timber wall does just that. The homeowners added patio space with brick pavers to extend their outdoor living up to the edge of the field.

Sun or shade? You have a choice when an upper deck extends over a patio. In the background, a collapsible patio umbrella provides the same sun-or-shade option.

Everything in this space defines the seating area. The owners enhanced what was open decking with a simple redwood planter housing a galvanized metal liner made in a sheet-metal shop.

A shift in the surface level helps define a nook framed by columns. The floor level links this sheltered space with the interior rooms.

The subtle colors of masonry materials seldom clash, lending themselves to more creative designs than you might think. Here, flagstone and brick— splashed with random pink pavers—provide an appealing patchwork that dramatically alters the drab expanse of an existing concrete slab.

Limestone slabs—cut and positioned precisely—add an air of Celtic mystery to this patio renovation.

DESIGNING FOR USEFULNESS

When the weather's right for outdoor dining, you'll want a place outside to make the meals. It reduces trips to the kitchen and keeps you close to your guests. This garden oasis, with sink and hearth, does double duty— providing a place to tend plants between picnics.

Even the most beautiful deck or patio won't be used much if, for example, it doesn't have convenient space for barbecuing or if dinner guests can't sit comfortably and talk. One way to enhance an area is to enlarge it strategically: Often, adding a small space in just the right spot can make a big difference. Whatever the nature of the improvement, begin by defining the problem; then design a plan that will solve it.

DEFINE YOUR NEEDS

Call a family meeting to get everyone's ideas about how they want to use the outdoors. Cooking and eating areas are primary. If you enjoy garden parties, you'll need conversation areas, too. Perhaps you need space for kids to play and a comfortable spot to read the paper.

How much space will you need? The best way to find out is to rope off the area and move in the furniture and equipment you will use—tables and chairs, barbecue equipment, and lounge furniture. Adjust the size until you get it right and then draw the plan on paper.

MAKING A DRAWING

No outdoor structure exists in isolation. You'll want your improved space to fit physically as well as aesthetically with the rest of your landscape. For that you'll need to make a map of your yard.

Draw the map on graph paper (¼ inch= 1 foot is a useful scale), and make several copies so you can experiment with different designs. First, make a rough sketch and mark the areas where different activities will take place. Then, make more detailed drawings, including specific pieces of furniture as well as built-in benches and planters.

PLANNING TIPS

Keep these points in mind as you plan any deck or patio project:
AREAS AND SIZES: Specific purposes have distinct space requirements. A cooking area, for example, should be about 6×10 feet. If you'll have one or two people helping, allow that much space for a preparation table.

A round or square table that seats four needs a 10×10-foot space; one with six or eight chairs needs a 12×12-foot space.

For lounging, allow a 4×6-foot space for each reclining chair. A conversation area about 9×9 feet will be suitable for a group of three to six people.

TRAFFIC FLOW: The above dimensions will feel cramped if people have to walk through them. Bypass those areas with pathways at least 3 feet wide.

ACCESS: Even when cooking outdoors, the food-preparation and dining spaces need to be near the kitchen. Locate outdoor cooking and dining areas (even the lounging area) close to the kitchen so you can move dinnerware and food quickly.

A PLEASING VIEW: When possible, orient furniture so you and your guests face the landscape. Be careful not to obstruct the view from the deck or from the kitchen window. Experiment with the positions of benches and planters so they don't hide the yard.

The height of deck railings needs careful consideration. For instance, if the deck surface is only slightly below the interior floor, a 42-inch railing may block the view completely. Lower the deck a step or two or install a railing that has clear acrylic panels.

SUN AND SHADE: Note the patterns of the sun and shade throughout the day and place the furniture accordingly. Where the sunlight is often too intense, build an overhead structure to provide shade where you need it (*see pages 42–53*).

WIND AND PRIVACY: If your site is in the path of uncomfortable winds, plan an attractive windbreak. A lattice fence with climbing plants or a tall hedge may work. Such additions also muffle street noise and hide unsightly views.

STORAGE: Make a list of implements and equipment you need to stow away, and plan storage that is easy to get to. The space under a deck may be ideal; install a skirt with a hinged door (*see pages 38–41*). Use caution when storing items that are subject to water damage—store them in waterproof containers placed in your below-deck storage area.

CHILDREN AT PLAY: If you have small children, position the play area where you can keep an eye on them while you read the paper in a lounge chair.

PLANTERS: Although they are small, flowers in pots or planters will brighten up the design. Place them where they attract attention but not where they obstruct the view.

These overhead structures add some much-needed shade. The posts, beams, clay roofing tiles, and exposed aggregate patio harmonize with the style of the house. And as with all successful outdoor alterations, they look like they've always been there.

Railings, benches, and screening have dual purposes. Here, they help frame a splendid view, but you also can use them to block unwanted sights and sounds. With planning, they offer panoramic views from any deck or patio.

Adobe pavers can be used in warm climates, bringing with them the look of the Southwest. Decorative tiles add a festive air. They make an ideal surface—not only for the patio and stairs, but for planters as well.

DESIGNING WITH WOOD

Just because lumber has square edges, you don't have to limit the design of your outdoor structures to shapes that are rigid and rectangular.

Versatile wood lends itself to artful design, asymmetrical shapes, and forms to complement your landscape architecture.

Decks may come to mind first when you think of lumber in an outdoor structure, but the uses of lumber are endless. It can be used to add privacy screens and planters, create ornate shapes for railings, build an ornamental trellis for climbing plants, or ease the transition between one area of the yard to another with wooden steps.

If you are extending a deck, the lumber you use will probably be similar to the existing structure. But, if you're planning a shade structure or a deck addition to a patio— or adding decorative elements not tied to the deck structure—your lumber choices become greater. Whatever the scope of your plans, here are some tips to keep in mind when making your selection.

CHOOSING THE RIGHT WOOD

Wood used in exterior structures must be rot-resistant. Pine, hemlock, or fir will start to fall apart after a few years if not treated or painted. These woods are fine if a painted surface complements your overall design and if you like how paint looks. But if you want the beauty of the wood grain revealed, you need a naturally-resistant species or pressure-treated wood.

REDWOOD: Beautiful and expensive, redwood is often used when cost is not an issue. There are many grades of redwood, each grade based on the larger number and size of knots that denote its strength.

Be careful! Not all redwood is long lasting. Dark heartwood will resist rot and insects, but cream-colored sapwood can be seriously damaged in just a couple of years. "Common" redwood, often sold as "construction common," is partially composed of sapwood. Grades that use the term "heart," such as "B heart" or "construction heart," are heartwood grades with some knots and are as rot resistant as heartwood grades that are "clear." Common redwood that has been treated is nearly as rot-resistant as pressure-treated lumber.

If you use heartwood, you can let redwood "go gray," meaning that you apply no stain and let it weather to a silvery color. (For staining options and techniques, see page 19.)

CEDAR: Less expensive than redwood, cedar has a lighter color and is generally regarded as less attractive. If you let it "go gray," it will not have quite the stately sheen of redwood. Because cedar does not have as many grades as redwood, its quality will vary within a grade. Don't rely on grading alone as an indication of quality. Inspect every board for knots and imperfections.

Only the darker-colored heartwood is rot-resistant. Unfortunately, most of the cedar sold today is sapwood, and many homeowners are dismayed to find their cedar decks rotting within a few years. If you use cedar for decking and rails, make sure it can dry out

Ironwood   Redwood   Cedar   Composition decking

between rainfalls, and give it a thorough coating of sealer/preservative.

IRONWOOD: If you have the budget, consider South American lumber species, such as ipé wood. It wears like iron, is extremely resistant to warping and rot, and requires little maintenance. A 1×4 of ironwood is actually stronger than a 2×4 of conventional wood such as fir, pine, or hemlock.

PRESSURE-TREATED LUMBER: Usually Douglas fir, Southern pine, or hemlock treated with chemicals under pressure, is the wood of choice for most decks and other outdoor structures. For posts and any structural member within 6 inches of the ground, get lumber with a "CCA" rating of .40 or greater or labeled for "ground contact." It will resist rotting even if it is continuously exposed to continual moisture for years.

Most pressure-treated wood has a green tint and, if left untreated, turns a dirty (not shiny) gray. However, you can purchase stains that are surprisingly convincing at making pressure-treated wood look like cedar. You also can purchase treated lumber that is brown, tinted to look like cedar.

COMPOSITION DECKING: Made of wood by-products, wood and plastic, or 100 percent plastic, composition materials offer long life and extreme rot and insect resistance. Most are suitable only for decking.

SELECTING THE BEST BOARDS

Visit the yard yourself and choose each board carefully. Don't just place an order and let the lumber yard drop off the deck wood. Make sure you can return unwanted boards for a full refund.

Check both sides of a board for knots. Small, tight knots usually will not come loose and do not weaken a board. A knot larger than 2 inches or that is loose or rough surfaced may pop out after a year or two.

Also check for warping. Pick up one end of the board and sight down its length. If you see a bad twist or bow (a curve along its length), don't buy it.

Inspect boards for cracks. A split more than 1 inch long will probably grow larger. But small hairline cracks—especially at the ends of the boards—can be cut off.

Store the lumber at home with stakes separating the boards to allow air circulation, and cover the stack with a tarp.

A lumber stamp tells you the lumber's grade (an indication of its quality), and its moisture content. For outdoor installation subject to moisture damage, look for "LP22," ".40 retention," or "ground contact." All indicate that a piece will survive wet conditions.

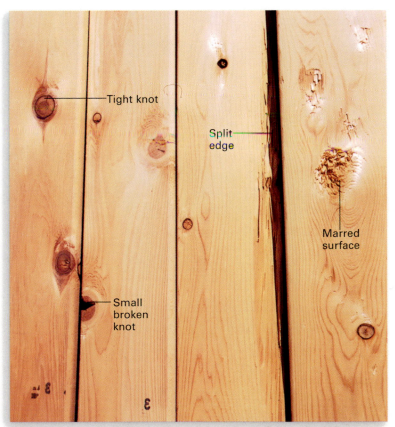

When you buy lumber, check each board carefully—don't buy boards by the lot. The defects shown here are cosmetic and won't impair structural soundness, but you'd want to hide them in the framing. Also, check the boards for cupping, twisting, and cracking.

DESIGNING WITH MASONRY

Masonry structures do not have to look stacked and squarish. Mix a variety of patterns, and throw in a swirl or two.

Most home centers carry a limited selection of the most popular bricks, pavers, tile, and stone. For something unusual, you may need to visit a brickyard or commercial masonry supplier. You'll find a wider variety of textures, shapes, and colors to inspire your imagination. You'll also find a full spectrum of prices, so shop carefully.

Set in a web of intersecting arcs, these paving bricks provide a fanciful complement to the curved wall. Finished brickwork requires an experienced mason but allows many ways to revive an existing patio.

BRICKS AND CONCRETE PAVERS

Bricks and pavers can lend an elegance to your landscape that no other material can quite match. Brick is modular—usually half as wide as it is long—which allows for easy material estimating and many pattern possibilities (*see page 23*). Precast concrete pavers, with their variety of shapes and forms, open up endless options for contoured designs. Both are virtually mistake proof when installed in a sand-laid patio.

BRICKS: These building staples vary greatly in color and texture, depending on the type of clay they are made of, how the blocks are cut, and how hot the kiln is when they are fired. Common brick can usually be used for walls and even patios in mild climates, but check the climate rating of the brick to make sure. If your winters are cold, or if a car will be driven over the surface, use paving bricks, which are harder and more resistant to cracking.

ADOBE: This traditional Southwestern material is made of fired clay. Its soft surface and light or off-red color invites relaxation. Outdoor use of adobe was once restricted to warm climates, but asphalt-reinforced adobe is now available that can stand up to freeze-thaw cycles in areas with mild winters.

PRECAST PAVERS: While they resemble brick, pavers are manufactured from concrete, making them stronger and less expensive than clay-fired brick. Many varieties are cast and colored to look like used common brick, and are available in many shapes—circles, squares, rectangles, diamonds, octagons, crescents, and more. You can join together interlocking pavers in repeating patterns. For variety, purchase pavers with variations in color.

Making circular or arcing patterns with pavers is especially easy using wedge-shaped, precast units of four or five different sizes. You simply start with the smallest size at the center and build the pattern a few rows at a time, adding rows of larger pieces as you go.

When you're choosing pavers, pay attention to scale. A small pattern can become too busy in a large area, but a small patio may seem dwarfed if the pavers are too large.

TURF BLOCK: This type of precast concrete paver made for planting comes in large pieces with a web or honeycomb design. Set turf block in soil that has been firmly tamped, fill the holes with soil, and allow grass or ground cover to grow through it. It will be strong enough to drive over.

STONE AND TILE

Stone always looks great next to a lawn or a tree, and it rarely clashes with the color scheme of a home. Natural stone comes in a wide variety of species and cuts, lending itself to free-form layouts and geometric patterns; types vary from region to region.

FLAGSTONE: Usually cut from limestone or other light-colored stone into thicknesses of up to 2 inches, flagstone is irregular in shape and has a rough surface. Like brick and pavers, it can be laid quickly in sand to form a surface that is beautiful (but perhaps too uneven for outdoor furniture). You also can set stone in tamped soil.

SLATE: A type of stone sliced into 1- to 2-inch thicknesses, slate is usually dark gray, but some varieties are light gray or reddish. Slate is somewhat brittle and should be set in mortar. "Vermont slate" comes in groups of variously sized rectangles that fit together like a puzzle.

LOOSE STONE: You can quickly build a casual border or garden path by pouring and tamping small stones in an excavated area. Suppliers usually carry various sizes and colors of small river rocks, crushed granite, and lava stones.

STONE FOR GARDEN WALLS: Rubble is uncut and has an irregular—but generally round—shape; cut-face stone has one smooth surface. Ashlar is stone cut into rectangular shapes of the same general thickness and is well-suited for simple, low garden walls.

TILE: Choose tile made for outdoor use, which usually means it will have an unglazed surface and will be at least ½ inch thick. (A glazed surface is dangerously slippery when wet.) Stone tile looks like natural stone but is cut into precise rectangles. Tile must be laid in mortar on top of a solid concrete slab.

A stunning stone-and-log bench rises from a limestone bed, encircled by upturned pavers. All materials are set in mortar on a concrete slab. Dark-colored grout emphasizes the random shapes of the limestone.

Be confident when mixing masonry materials. Here, variously colored slate rectangles are accented with brick paver insets.

Masonry adapts to elegant sculptural forms. Hard, cool, and smooth, it contrasts with the landscape. The grid of plants and pavers provides a transition between patio and garden.

A sharp eye and minimal grading turned unused yard into overflow space for parties. Grey stone contrasts nicely with airy balusters.

BUILDING CODES

The building department in your area has regulations that may apply to a deck or patio project. Find out setback requirements so you will not build too close to the property line. You may need to comply with rules governing the sizes of structural members of a deck, and there may be very specific rules regarding railings. Patio structures may also have to meet requirements to ensure strength, stability, and longevity.

DECK AND PATIO FACE-LIFTING MAKEOVERS

Whether you want to replace an existing outdoor surface that's in bad shape or add an extension to it, this chapter will guide you through the steps for upgrading your outdoor living space. You will find all the basic steps for deck and patio construction plus tips for adding on to existing structures.

As long as you pay attention to basic structural requirements, you'll have much latitude in the design of your upgrade. For example, when extending a structure, feel free to use a surface material that varies from the old. Differences in material, pattern, and color often add character.

If your existing deck is sound but drab, try cleaning and staining it (see pages 18–19). If the joists, beams, and posts are in good shape but the decking is not, consider removing the

decking only and replacing it with new material, perhaps running in a different direction. You may have to add a few structural pieces to support the decking; if so, follow instructions on page 17.

An ordinary-looking concrete slab can be an asset: If it is stable and strong (see page 23) you can resurface it with tiles or stones set in a bed of mortar. You can even break up the surface of the concrete to simulate flagstones.

To build a deck extension, you may be able to tie new joists to the existing beams. If that's not feasible, just build a new deck next to the old one. To add adjoining patio space, excavate and lay a new surface. You may need to remove some of the existing patio edging and move it over.

DO IT YOURSELF OR HIRE A PROFESSIONAL?

Costs for contracting outdoor improvements will roughly be twice the cost of materials. That means you may be able to cut your costs in half by doing the work yourself. Before you make the plunge, consider these points:

■ Do you enjoy physical labor and have some carpentry or outdoor projects under your belt? If not, you will probably work slowly; it may make more sense to hire a pro.

■ You can probably get about the same prices for lumber as a professional gets. Lumberyards often discount, depending on the volume of sale. A contractor may get a better price for

masonry materials, however, because masonry suppliers discount to those with whom they do a regular business.

■ If the site for your deck or patio is steep, if you need a deck raised more than 8 feet above the ground, or if you need to support a heavy structure such as a spa, hire a professional who has successfully completed several similar projects.

■ Still unsure? Get bids from contractors. Then weigh the expense of a professional job against your cost of materials and the value of your time.

EXPANDING A DECK

Closely examine the structure of your existing deck to determine how to build an extension. If the existing deck is strong, you can probably build an extension that uses the same kinds of materials in similar configurations. Your local building department can confirm this when you apply for a permit.

START WITH A LEDGER

A ledger is a joist—the one that attaches the deck to your house. If your deck extension will adjoin the house, start the construction with a ledger. If the extension will attach elsewhere on the existing deck, you'll start with a header, end joist, or beam. Fasten the new joists with joist hangers, positioning them at the same level as your existing deck, or above or below it (*see page 17*).

POSITIONING THE LEDGER: Place a ledger so the deck surface will be 1 inch below the door sill when you walk out onto the deck. That will keep rain, snow, and leaves out of the house. For 2× decking, locate the ledger 2½ inches below the interior floor— 2 inches if you are using ⁵⁄₄-inch decking.

KEEP IT DRY: Rainwater that collects between the ledger and house will eventually rot the siding and the ledger. Use flashing or washers to keep the ledger joint dry (see illustrations below).

ATTACHING THE LEDGER: The ledger must be level, plumb, straight, and firmly attached. On a frame house, drive 5-inch lag screws into studs or every 16 inches in the band joist—not just the siding. When attaching to masonry, use masonry anchors and lag screws.

ADD FOOTINGS AND POSTS

Whether your deck extension has started with a ledger or with other structural members of the deck, the next step is laying out footings. You'll want the extension square to the house or to the existing deck—if it isn't, framing will be difficult and the deck will look awkward. Here's how to get things right.

LAYING OUT FOR SQUARE: Before digging the footing holes, put temporary stakes at the corners of your extension. In most cases, you'll want the joists to extend a foot or two beyond the beam (see the illustration on page 15) so allow for that measurement when setting the stakes.

Drive batter boards (pointed 2×4s with a 2×4 crosspiece) in the ground 2 feet or so beyond the stakes. Stretch mason's lines from the ledger (or other structural member) to the batter boards in all directions—these lines represent the outside surfaces of the end and header joists.

Square the lines with the time-honored 3-4-5 method (see illustration, opposite). Suspend a plumb bob at the intersection of the lines and mark the spot with a nail and piece of paper.

Measure in diagonally from the nail about 4½ inches and mark that spot with another nail. Have a helper hold a post in position— its faces should be 1½ inches from the mason's lines. Repeat the process at each corner. Once you are sure of each post's location, you're ready to dig footings.

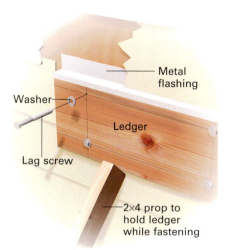

If your house has beveled siding, use a circular saw to cut out the ledger recess ½ inch wider and 3 inches longer than the ledger (so the end joists will fit at the ends). Tuck metal flashing under the siding and attach the ledger with lag screws.

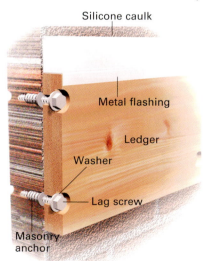

Use lag screws and masonry anchors to attach a ledger to a brick or concrete surface. Caulk the flashing with silicone caulk.

To provide air circulation, use four or five washers as spacers. Drive lag screws through the siding and at least 2 inches into a framing member.

THE 3-4-5 METHOD

From a corner, mark one of the lines at 3 feet (use a bit of tape), and the other line (or the ledger) at 4 feet. If the distance between the marks is 5 feet, the corner is square. Test all of the corners.

USE THE RIGHT LUMBER SIZE

The span of a board is the distance from one point of support to the next point of support. Local building departments have specific span requirements; check with them before deciding whether to use 2×8 or 2×10 joists. Here are some guidelines for building a deck that will feel firm and will not sag after a few years.

If the joists are spaced 16 inches apart, a 2×6 should span no more than 9 feet; a 2×8, no more than 12 feet; a 2×10, no more than 15 feet.

If the joists are spaced 24 inches apart, a 2×6 should span no more than 8 feet; a 2×8, no more than 10 feet; and a 2×10, no more than 12½ feet.

A 4×6 beam (or a beam made of two 2×6s joined together) should span no more than 6 feet; a 4×8, no more than 8 feet; and a 4×12, no more than 9 feet.

ELEMENTS OF A DECK

Your deck may differ from the drawing on this page, but most of the parts will be similar.

FOOTINGS AND POSTS: Deck posts (usually 4×4s) must rest on concrete footings extending below the frost line.

BEAMS: Beams (single 4× lumber, or two or three pieces of 2×) must be strong enough to support the entire deck.

LEDGER: A single 2× that anchors the deck to the house.

JOISTS AND FASCIA: Joists are 2× lumber spaced either 16 or 24 inches apart that support the decking. A header joist is perpendicular to the others. Outer joists are called end joists. Headers and end joists are sometimes covered with attractive 1× fascia.

DECKING: Most commonly 2×4, 2×6, or ⁵/₄×6 lumber, decking is attached to the joists.

RAILINGS: Regardless of style, most railings have 4×4 posts, top and bottom rails, balusters, and a cap plate.

DECK AND EXTENSION

EXPANDING A DECK
continued

If your winters are mild, you may opt for this type of footing. Dig a hole about 18 inches deep and add 6 inches of gravel. Pour concrete over the gravel base, set the precast pier in it, and check for level.

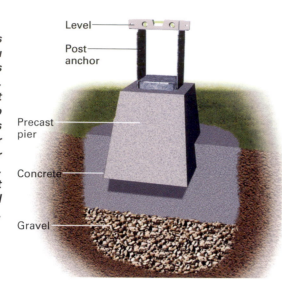

Level

Post anchor

Precast pier

Concrete

Gravel

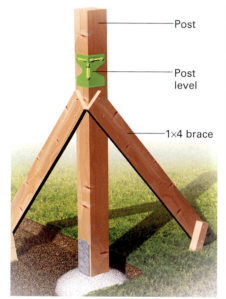

Post

Post level

1×4 brace

Anchor each post with 1×4 staked braces. Use a post level or a carpenter's level on adjacent sides to plumb the post.

Attach the end joists to the ledger and rest them on the beam. Have a helper or two hold the header joist while you attach it to the end joists.

"CROWN SIDE UP"

Most boards are not perfectly straight. If you look down the length of one, you'll see that it bends a bit. The top of the bend is called the "crown." For the sake of strength and to ensure against a wavy surface, check each board to make sure that all joists and beams are installed with the crown facing up.

DIGGING AND POURING FOOTINGS:

Check with your building department to find out the type and depth of footing for your climate and soil. If you have cold winters, a concrete footing should reach below the frost line. Otherwise, the footing—and the deck—will rise and fall with the "frost heave."

If you only have a few holes, use a clamshell digger. For more extensive work, rent a power auger. When the footing is dug, shovel in 4 inches of gravel for drainage, and insert a concrete tube form supported about 1 inch above grade. Fill the hole with concrete.

POST ANCHORS: While the concrete is wet, insert a post anchor or J-bolt into it (so you can attach a post anchor later). Choose an adjustable anchor so you can shift the position of the post slightly.

SET THE POSTS: Install posts that are taller than they need to be; you will trim them later. Brace them plumb (see illustration at left, center), and recheck for square.

FRAMING

Use 16 penny (16d) galvanized nails or 3-inch decking screws to attach most framing pieces. Attach joist hangers with hanger nails or 1¼-inch decking screws.

CUT THE POSTS: Using a water level, mark one post at a point level with the top of the ledger (or the member you'll attach the joists to). Measure down from that line the depth of the joist, and again by the width of the beam if the beam will sit on top of the post. Cut the post at the mark with a circular saw. Measure and cut the other posts the same way.

INSTALL THE BEAM: The beam will usually be 3 inches longer than the ledger (because 1½-inch end joists will be attached to both ends of the ledger). Cut the beam (a 4×

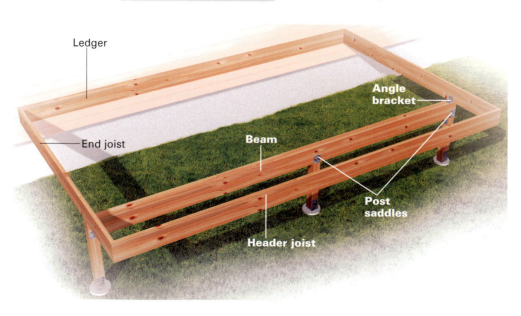

Ledger

End joist

Angle bracket

Beam

Post saddles

Header joist

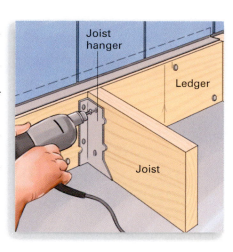

Space joists evenly and attach them with joist hangers. Use a scrap piece of joist material to position the hangers, and attach them with nails or screws.

To add a new decking surface that is lower than the existing deck, tie the new joists to the beam with joist hangers. If the existing joists are 2×8s, you will have a comfortable 7¼-inch step down.

member or three 2× members nailed together) to length. Set the beam on top of the posts and attach it with post saddles.

LAYOUT FOR THE JOISTS: Starting at the edge of the ledger recess, mark the ledger every 16 or 24 inches (depending on local codes). Cut the header joist to the same length as the ledger and, holding it up against the ledger, duplicate the marks.

BUILD THE FRAMING: Rest each end joist on the beam, and attach them to the end of the ledger with nails or screws and an angle bracket. Attach the header joist to the end joists (have a helper hold the header).

Now fill in the middle joists. First, install joist hangers centered on your marks on the ledger and header joist. (Hold a short piece of joist-sized scrap in a hanger, flush with the top of the header or ledger, and attach the hanger with nails or screws.) Install all the hangers the same way.

Measure and cut the joists to length; with a helper, slide each joist in the hanger with its crown edge up. Drive nails or screws through the joist hangers and into the joists. Square the frame and toenail or screw the joists to the beam.

FRAMING FOR NEW DECK EXTENSION

To frame a new deck surface a step higher than the original, set the framing on top. In this case, 2×6 joists are ideal. With 1½ inch-thick decking on top of them, you will have a 7-inch step up.

DECKING

All the decking must be supported by a framing member. If possible, use lumber long enough to span the deck extension without joints. Otherwise, stagger the joints and center them on a joist (lay out the decking first so you can arrange the pattern).

Install the first board at the end of the deck that is most visible. That way, you can make minor spacing adjustments where they'll be least noticeable. Chalk a perpendicular line along the top of the joists so the decking will be straight; use 8d nails as spacers to create an ⅛-inch gap between the boards.

If the wood is wet, (pressure-treated lumber often is), butt the pieces together—they will

shrink within a year. Let the decking overhang the joists. They don't have to be even at this stage; you will cut them to an even overhang later.

Every fourth or fifth board, use a line to check that the boards are square. If you need to straighten a board, use a flat pry bar to push or pull the errant edge into line. Rip-cut the last board to fit the remaining opening. When all the boards are installed, snap a chalk line so the decking overhangs 1½ inches (2¼ inches if you're installing a 1× fascia) beyond the outside joist or fascia. Cut with a circular saw set to the depth of the decking.

When all the decking boards are attached, snap a chalk line and cut with a circular saw.

MAINTAINING, CLEANING, AND REFINISHING A DECK

Wood rots when it can't dry out— and rot is usually hidden from view. Check the underside of stair treads, stringers, and decking, and the tops and bottoms of the posts. Poke the wood with a screwdriver. If it feels spongy, rot has begun, but you may be able to stop it with a sealer. A half inch of soft wood may require replacement of the rotted member.

Stair stringers are especially susceptible to rot. Here, the joint between the stringer and the deck has rotted, causing a hazard. Another area prone to rot is just below the treads, where they rest on a part of the stringer that has been cut.

Before you decide to make extensive— and expensive—changes to your deck, consider the easiest solution. Cleaning and refinishing can give a drab deck a fresh new look—you'll be surprised how much bigger it looks, too—and may change your mind about making major modifications. Before you start, however, make sure your deck is structurally sound.

INSPECT A DECK FOR DAMAGE: Once a year, tighten loose fasteners and check your deck for damaged wood. Most rot occurs in areas that are not easily visible, such as under the decking and at the bottom of posts. To check for rot, poke the lumber with a screwdriver; if it slides in easily, you have a problem. Check joists and beams: They're not as likely to rot but are subject to cracks.

REPLACE DAMAGED BOARDS: If a deck board is split or is splintering, remove it. To avoid damaging adjoining boards, remove the fasteners first. Use a "cat's paw" to pull out nails, or a drill equipped with a screwdriver bit to remove screws.

If a joist is damaged, instead of replacing it, add a new piece to the old one. Nail or screw the new joist to the old one, and toenail it to the structural member at both ends. If a beam, post, or ledger is badly damaged, call in a professional carpenter.

DEALING WITH ROT: Sitting moisture is the worst enemy of wood. Most deck problems occur because moisture stays on the wood for extended periods of time. Prevent rot by encouraging air circulation. Simply raking leaves away is a good way to start.

Wood that is spongy will only grow weaker over time if the problem is not addressed. If a joist is not badly rotted, treat it with sealer/preservative to prevent further damage and nail another board alongside it. If the rot is extensive, support the structure and remove and replace the board. Once you start removing boards, you may find that other boards have hidden rot. You may need to replace the entire section of the deck.

TESTING WATER RESISTANCE: If the surface is dry, it will soak up water like a sponge, causing not only rot but also cracking when the boards go through freeze-thaw or wet-dry cycles. Sprinkle a little water on your deck. If it beads up, the boards are protected. If the water soaks in within a minute, you need a sealer.

CLEANING A DECK: Many neglected decks get mildewed, covered with algae, or take on a dingy gray. This usually is only a surface problem, which a good cleaning will remedy.

Wash the deck with hot water and a stiff brush, or rent a pressure-washer (use a fan tip so you will not tear up the surface). To remove algae, see page 24.

If simple washing does not do the job, or if you want the deck lightened so you can apply an attractive finish, purchase a deck cleaning product. If the wood is in very bad shape, use oxalic acid, which is mixed with water. Scrub the area with a stiff natural bristle brush, rinse, allow it to dry, and repeat if necessary. Wear protective clothing—oxalic acid is extremely caustic.

HIRING PROFESSIONAL CLEANERS

You can find deck-cleaning companies in the Yellow Pages in many areas. Call around for prices and get a list of references. Visit decks the professionals have cleaned and finished—decks made of the same lumber as yours. If you find just the right finish and color you are looking for, ask the company to do the same for your deck.

SEALERS, STAINS, AND PAINT

All wood surfaces hold up best when protected with some kind of finish. The product you use will depend on the color, tone, and surface sheen your want, as well as the durability and ease of application.

SEALERS: Sealers provide protection from water damage and won't appreciably change the appearance of your deck. Look for sealers that contain oil or paraffin, a UV blocker to keep the sun from turning your deck gray, and an insecticide.

STAINS: Either water or oil based, stains won't provide the moisture protection of sealers. They are useful, however, when you want a color that harmonizes with the rest of your design and shows off the natural beauty of the wood. They are easily applied over rough surfaces. Semitransparent stains highlight the grain; some heavy-bodied stains are as opaque as paint, hiding the grain but not defects.

PAINT: Paint—whether oil or water-based—requires a primer. Properly applied, paint covers minor defects and lasts longer than other finishes. Generally more expensive than other finishes, paints are available in a wide variety of colors and sheens. An acrylic-latex topcoat over an alkyd primer is very durable.

Wood that has turned gray usually can be brought back to life by washing with a deck cleaner or a wood bleach. Once you have cleaned it, apply stain or sealer within a few days to prevent the gray from returning.

INSTALLING A SAND-LAID PATIO

Masonry materials mix and match well, so feel confident to use surface or edging materials that differ from the existing patio. Different materials can complement each other pleasingly. Here are the basics for adding a sand-laid patio, using whatever masonry materials you choose.

Edging provides a frame for a patio surface, keeping sand-laid bricks or pavers from wandering. To install 4×4 or 6×6 landscaping timbers, excavate and tamp a level trench and lay in the timber. Every 2 feet or so, drill a hole and drive a 16-inch piece of rebar into the ground to anchor the timber.

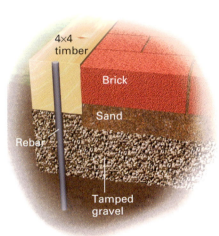

For wood edging, use redwood or pressure-treated 2×4s or 2×6s set on a gravel bed. Pound in pressure-treated or metal stakes every foot or so to hold the lumber in place.

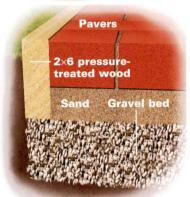

LAY OUT AND INSTALL EDGING

In most regions, you'll need a 4-inch gravel base covered with a 2-inch sand bed for a patio base. The gravel provides drainage to minimize the effects of ground heaving caused by freeze-thaw cycles.

If you have firm and well-drained soil, you may not need a gravel base, but check with builders in your area to make sure. If your patio will be large, excavate most of the area before installing edging. Hire someone to help dig with shovels, or rent a small excavating machine.

Before you begin the steps below, remove any existing edging where the new paving surface will adjoin against the old. If you're keeping the old edging in place and it starts to fall into your new excavation, prop or stake it in place until you lay the new base.

MARKING THE PERIMETER WITH EDGING: Use stakes or batter boards with mason's lines to establish a site that is square. Check it with the 3-4-5 method (*see page 15*).

Lay lumber or other edging material on the ground, and dig a trench 2 inches wider and 2 to 3 inches deeper than the material itself. Add a gravel base to the trench and tamp it down. Set in the edging and adjust the gravel until the edging is at the height you want. (Positioning the edging an inch or so above ground level will make mowing easier—your mower will ride on the edge, cutting the grass to about the same height.) Make sure the edging is properly sloped for drainage.

SLOPING THE EDGING: The patio (and edging) should slope about ¼ inch per running foot away from the house. If the edging is made of lumber or landscaping timbers, adjust the slope with a carpenter's level. If you use brick soldiers for edging, run lines that are square and correctly sloped, and install the soldiers under the line. You also can quickly check with scrap 1× stock placed just under the downslope end of a 4-foot carpenter's level. (See illustration, opposite.)

In either case, add or remove sand, soil, or gravel under the edging until it reaches the correct slope.

Align brick soldiers on a bed of sand or concrete. Tap them with a rubber mallet to straighten the row.

Install plastic edging for a curved patio. It's faster and easier than home-made forms.

A simple way to check the slope of the edging is to just set a scrap of 1× lumber flat under the downslope end of a 4-foot level. When the level's bubble is centered, the edging is sloped at nearly ¼ inch per running foot. Use a grid of mason's lines and a shovel marked with tape to make sure you are excavating to the proper depth.

EXCAVATE THE INTERIOR: Dig away all the turf, and remove any roots larger than ½ inch in diameter. If you cut the sod neatly and roll it, you can reuse it elsewhere.

Excavate to the depth required for the installation—2 inches plus the depth of the paving for a sand-only bed, 6 inches plus the brick thickness for a gravel-and-sand setting.

To keep the excavation level throughout, stretch a grid of properly sloped mason's line every 4 feet across the entire area. Fasten the lines directly to wood edging with nails, or use stakes to stretch them across the top of brick edging. Measure down periodically as you dig.

To get started, mark your shovel with tape to indicate the correct depth. Avoid overdigging and disturbing the soil at the bottom of the excavation.

TAMP THE SOIL: Use a rented vibrating compactor to compact the soil. The more thoroughly you tamp, the firmer the patio will be. Check the edging again to make sure it has not been bumped out of alignment.

LAYING THE GRAVEL AND SAND SUBSTRATE

Setting the bricks or pavers will be easier if the sand substrate is smooth and even; if it is not smooth, you will invite disaster. Take the time to do the job right.

LAY A GRAVEL BASE: Remove the mason's-line grid. If you have chosen to reinforce your patio with gravel, have the delivery truck dump it inside the excavated area if possible, being careful not to disturb the edging. Spread the gravel first with shovels, then with a heavy rake. Reattach the mason's lines to check for uniform depth. (You also can drive small stakes into the ground to a 4-inch height before you bring in the gravel.) Tamp the gravel, adding and tamping until the base is at the correct depth.

LAYING FLAGSTONE IN TAMPED SOIL

Flagstone can be set in sand using the methods described for brick and pavers or it can simply be laid on top of tamped soil. You also can use the technique to lay a walk with soil-based flagstone; set the stones in place in the pattern of your choice, dig around the outline, and set as for a patio.

No edging is necessary. Excavate all turf and organic material from the patio area. Rake the surface until it is even; tamp it firm and rake again.

Arrange the stones in a pattern that evenly mixes small stones with larger stones. Spend time testing various patterns until you find groupings with fairly even joint lines.

When a group of six or seven stones is configured, stand on each one. If it wobbles, pick it up and either dig away or add soil in order to stabilize the base. Take your time getting each stone level and stable; a wobble today won't go away.

Use uncut stones as much as possible. If you need to cut a stone, use a small sledge and a brickset. First, score a shallow cut line across the stone. Then, place a metal pipe or a board under the cut line and give it a solid whack with the sledge.

When the stones are laid, carefully shovel soil into the joints. Spray the entire surface with a light mist, then fill in any resulting low spots. Allow grass to grow in the joints, or plant low-growing ground cover.

INSTALLING A SAND-LAID PATIO
continued

ADD LANDSCAPING FABRIC: Cover the area with landscaping fabric to keep weeds from growing through the new patio surface while allowing water to drain through.

BUILD GUIDES AND A SCREED: To smooth the sand to a uniform depth, you will need a screed—a 2×6 notched to the thickness of your pavers (see illustration below). If the patio is 8 feet wide or less, use the edging as a guide for the screed, setting the "ears" of the screed on the edging. If the patio is wider, install one or more staked upright 2×4s as temporary screed guides.

SCREEDING THE SAND: Have sand dumped into the patio area, and spread it with shovels. Dampen the sand with a fine mist. Draw the screed towards you, pulling one side slightly then the other. Dampen again, fill in any low spots, and screed again. Avoid walking on the screeded sand. Then tamp it and check for the correct depth.

SETTING THE PAVERS

Place precast pavers tightly together (they will have tabs to keep them at the correct spacing). However, bricks are placed with about a ⅛-inch gap between them. Do not kneel in the screeded sand; work from outside the patio, or use a kneeling board to only kneel on the newly laid paver surface.

PLACE THE PAVERS: Lay the bricks or pavers in the pattern of your choice, starting in a corner and working outward. If you use plastic edging, each paver should fit snugly against it. With other edging material, leave an ⅛-inch gap between it and the pavers.

Push each brick straight down into place. Don't slide it—you'll dislodge the sand. Give each brick a light tap with a rubber mallet (or use a hammer on a scrap piece of wood). As you work, keep checking the surface for level and slope: Cut a 2×4 to the correct slope and

Sand

Screed board

Kneeling board

2×4 with level

Sand

Place a bit more sand than you need in the area to be screeded, then drag the screed board across to achieve a smooth, even surface. The screed board is notched so that the finished sand surface will be a paver-thickness below the edging. Use a mallet to gently tap each paver into place. Use a short piece of 2×4 spanning several pavers to make sure they form an even surface; tap with the mallet if needed. By sweeping fine sand into the cracks, you not only improve the appearance of the patio but also increase its strength dramatically. When packed into the joints, the sand wedges the pavers together.

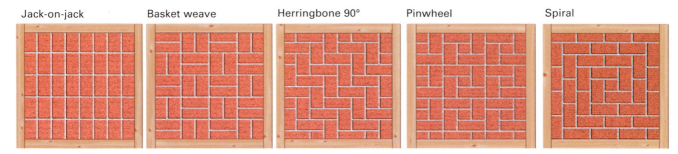

| Jack-on-jack | Basket weave | Herringbone 90° | Pinwheel | Spiral |

The jack-on-jack pattern is easy to lay and is charming, but consider other paver patterns as well.

use it under a carpenter's level (*see page 21*). When the bubble centers, the slope is right.

When there are a few bricks from the opposite edging, stretch a taut line to measure for straightness and for the correct height. If the surface is low in some places, remove the pavers, add more sand, tamp, and then replace the pavers. If some spots are a bit high, adjust the paver height either with a few sharp taps from the mallet or by scraping out sand and replacing the pavers.

CUT BRICKS: Install all the full bricks, then measure for the bricks that need to be cut. If you only have a few to cut, you can use a brickset and mallet, but that is slow work. For quick and precise cuts, rent a wet masonry saw like the one at right.

FILL THE JOINTS WITH SAND: Shovel some fine, dry sand on top of the paver surface. Sweep with a broom in several directions so the sand will seep down into all the cracks. Spray the entire surface with a fine mist to soak the sand. Allow the sand to dry and then spread more dry sand. Run a vibrating compactor over the paver surface to give it a final compacting, and reapply dry sand.

STONE IN SAND SURFACES

Setting flagstone in a sand base requires the same methods as brick in sand. You'll have to spend a bit more time laying out the pattern. Experiment on the ground outside the area, visualizing sections, not individual stones. Vary the sizes, shapes, and colors until you have created a pattern that you like.

Rent a wet masonry saw to quickly produce professional-quality cuts in bricks or pavers.

MORTARED BRICK PATIO

A mortared brick patio will provide years of trouble-free enjoyment, but its installation requires considerably more effort and expense. You will actually be building two patios— a concrete slab to provide the brick with a solid base and the brick surface itself.

Concrete slabs (3 or 4 inches thick) call for a gravel base of an equal depth. When the slab has cured, the brick is laid in a 1-inch mortar bed and the gaps filled with mortar. This project requires a moderate amount of masonry skill and a crew of helpers, but is within the means of most do-it-yourselfers.

CAN YOU USE THE OLD SLAB?

You can lay a new patio surface on an old concrete slab if the slab is in good condition. If the base is inadequate, it's time to pull it out. Check for large cracks and sagging sections—good indications the base is not adequate. Next, dig a hole or two along the perimeter at each side. If you have a 4-inch gravel base and 4 inches of concrete, the slab is fine for resurfacing or mortaring brick or stone.

Then check the surface. It should be sloped for drainage— at least 1 inch for every 4 feet. For mortared brick, tile, or stone, the existing surface should not have high spots of more than 1/8-inch in 10 feet. A surface that is gradually crowned in the center is fine for mortaring. Repair minor holes or flaking and replace loose or damaged brick and tile.

MAINTAINING MASONRY FINISHES

Cracked flagstone lets you be selective about your patio repairs—you don't have to remove the entire surface. Pry up the cracked stone with a crowbar and replace it with one of similar shape and size.

Algae can grow quickly on outdoor surfaces and, in addition to its unsightly appearance, becomes slippery and dangerous underfoot. Scrubbing with a solution of household bleach, laundry soap, water, and trisodium phosphate (TSP) will return the patio to its original condition.

Don't change your patio just because it shows some minor wear and tear. If it's in relatively good shape—and you like its location and looks—a little maintenance may prolong its useful life.

KEEPING THE PUDDLES AWAY: Don't let water stand on your patio after a rainfall—keep it from collecting in the first place. Water between or soaked into bricks or stones can cause serious cracking when it freezes.

Take a look at your patio after a rain. If you have puddles on the bricks, or the puddles at the edges don't dry up after a day, you can do something to prevent damage.

The solution may be as simple as redirecting a gutter downspout away from the patio. If the puddles are at the perimeter of the patio, dig a drainage trench and fill it with gravel or wood chips.

If perimeter puddles stay for days, you need a serious drainage system. Dig a trench sloping away from the house and ending in a large gravel-filled dry well. Line the trench with gravel and perforated drainpipe leading to the well.

Puddles may occur because of an inadequate slope. Remove bricks or pavers that are causing a small dip, add sand, and reinstall them so that water runs off.

APPLYING SEALER: Concrete pavers and flagstones are strong and not very absorbent, so they usually do not need a sealer. Unglazed bricks may be sponge-like, so an application of clear masonry sealer could help. Apply the sealer with a paint brush or roller, or use a pump-sprayer.

PATIO MAINTENANCE

Sand-set bricks, pavers, and flagstones usually wear well and don't require much attention. If the edging and base have been properly installed, you need do no more than keep it well swept, perhaps pull an occasional weed, and refill the joints with sand every year or two (see page 22).

REMOVING MOSS AND ALGAE: Mix a solution of 1 ounce laundry soap, 3 ounces trisodium phosphate (or a nonphosphate TSP substitute), 1 quart chlorine bleach, and 3 quarts water. Brush it on, let it sit for five minutes, and rinse. TSP is caustic, so wear rubber gloves and eye protection.

CLEANING STAINS: Most grease and oil stains will come out by scrubbing with laundry detergent and warm water. If a stain has penetrated deeply, saturate it with mineral spirits and cover it with dry portland cement or cat litter. Let it stand overnight, then sweep it away. For more stubborn stains, try a paste of benzol and cat litter or cement. Let it stand for an hour and repeat if necessary.

REPLACING BRICK OR STONE: Pry up a heaved or damaged brick or flagstone with a flat prybar, or with two putty knives: one at each end. Moisten the sand and reset the unit, tapping it with a rubber mallet. If it's still high, scrape a little sand out and reset it. If you can't get a damaged piece out with a prybar, break it up with a cold chisel. Drive it with a baby sledge—pavers are hard. Then moisten and tamp the sand (use a 2×4) and set in new brick or stone. Fill the joints with sand as you would for a new patio.

CONCRETE MAINTENANCE

Wash concrete surfaces occasionally with laundry soap and water, or try the solutions described above for cleaning brick and stone. Scrub tough stains with a stiff push broom or scrub brush. (Don't use wire brushes on smooth concrete—the metal will scratch the surface.) Use muriatic acid to etch away stains that won't come out with standard cleaners. Mix 1 part acid to 9 parts water. Wear rubber gloves, old clothes, and eye protection—muriatic acid is highly caustic. Scrub the mixture into the area with a stiff brush and let it stand five to 10 minutes. Rinse thoroughly.

REPAIRING CONCRETE: Concrete will suffer from dusting (the surface wears away easily), scaling (the surface flakes), spalling (deeper scaling), crazing (a fine network of surface cracks) and pop-outs (small holes).

Except for pop-outs, you can clean the area (see illustration above), brush on a latex bonding agent, and trowel on a thin layer of concrete patch (a mixture of vinyl, portland cement, and sand), feathering its edges.

Here's a better solution for all these problems that also will work for cracks wider than ⅛ inch. Break out the affected surface with a small sledge and cold chisel to a depth of ½ to ¾ inch. Holding the chisel at an angle, key the outside edge of the area to be repaired, making it bigger on the bottom than the top. Keying a repair helps lock the patch in place. Thoroughly remove all dust and concrete particles—a shop vacuum will do this quickly. Wet the surface with a latex concrete bonding agent and trowel on a layer of concrete patch. Smooth the surface with a steel trowel and texture it to match the surrounding area.

Cold chisel

Trowel

Crack "keyed" to keep patch from popping out

Chisel a "key" in a crack, and press patching concrete into the hole. Trowel the surface smooth.

Damaged area

Circular saw

If a large area has surface damage, cut its outline to a depth of ¾ inch or so, using a circular saw with a masonry blade. Chisel out the interior, brush on a latex bonding agent, and fill the hole with sand-mix concrete. Trowel smooth.

BREAKING UP THE SURFACE

If the concrete slab is beyond repair, think through removing it yourself. Breaking up concrete is heavy work. You will need at least a 10-pound sledge—heavier if you can handle it—and crowbars.

Crack small sections, starting at a corner. Pry the section out with a crowbar (pry against the unbroken concrete, not against the surrounding soil) and carry it off in a wheelbarrow. Work your way across the surface, cracking it and prying—the crowbar should do the work. If the slab is thicker than 4 inches, or the patio surface is large, use a rented masonry saw or jackhammer. Work safely using heavy gloves, steel toed-boots, and safety goggles.

Sand-set brick and stone give up more easily. Pry up a corner, remove the pieces, and set them aside to use on your new surface if they're not damaged.

Railings express a deck's personality. Often, railings are used to reflect elements of a home's architecture. This railing's balusters get elegant, massive scale by boxing posts in a wooden frame. The post caps, railings, and ornamental balusters are all made with common dimensional lumber.

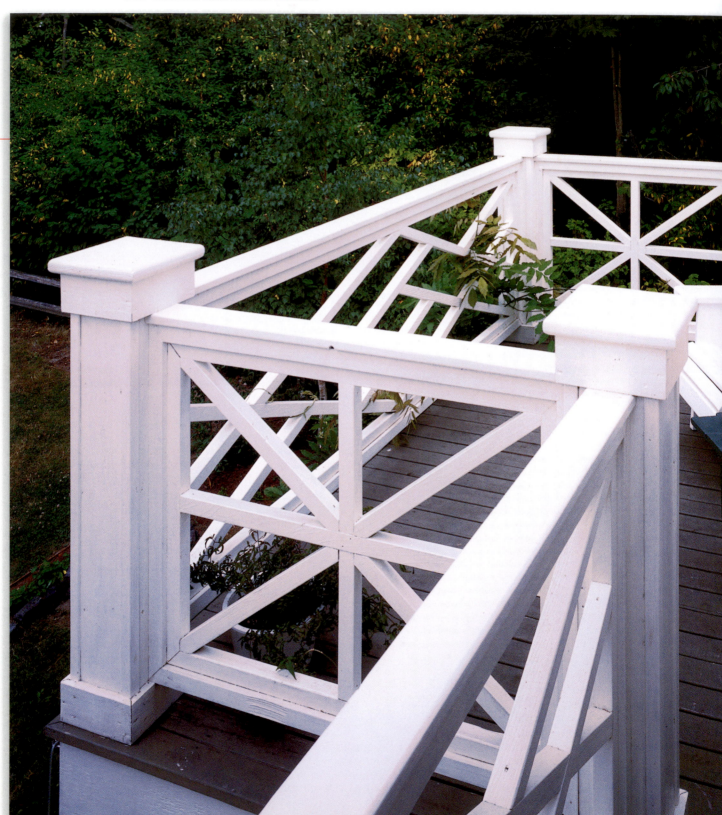

RAILINGS, SKIRTS, AND STAIRS

Most of the energy and money spent on a deck is for the horizontal surface—building the structure and applying decking. But the most noticeable features to anyone passing by are vertical—the railing, the skirting under the deck, and the stairway. You often can dramatically improve the appearance for a modest cost by changing the vertical elements.

Even a plain railing on a low-budget deck has the basic building blocks—posts, top, and bottom rail—for a stylish upgrade. Install evenly spaced balusters, latticework, or acrylic panels. Top the posts with decorative caps, or cut them to a point. If you have no rail cap or if yours is just a 2×4, install a spacious 2×8 cap where you can conveniently place potted plants and drinks.

If your deck is so high that you can look into its understructure, adding a skirt will hide the joists and add an appealing architectural detail. Make a door in the skirt for access to a great place to store garden equipment.

Stairways can make a statement too. Replace a simple 3-foot-wide stairway with one that is 4 or 5 feet wide with extra-wide treads. You will have plenty of overflow seating at parties and a dramatic feature that will enhance your deck's appeal.

Add all three—railing, skirt, and stairway— to transform the appearance and comfort of your outdoor living space.

IMAGINATIVE RAILINGS

This railing combines several whimsical elements. Posts are massive 6×6s with 2×4 rails and 2×3 balusters. The newels (pieces on top of the posts) are in two parts, both purchased at a deck supply yard. The top rails are 4×4s wrapped with corrugated plastic drainpipe. To be sure they fit exactly, the curved purple metal rod partitions were custom made and anodized by a metal fabricator after the rest of the railing was built.

This redwood deck and railing were stained to enhance the beauty of the wood. The 4×4 "through-posts" carry all the way to the ground, so they support the structure as well as the railing. The top and bottom rails are 2×4s, and the balusters are alternating 2×2s and 1×6s.

Log railings were a natural choice for this house. Building a railing like this involves a special carpentry technique: Large mortises—conforming to the shape of the logs—are bored into the supports to hold the ends of logs or tenons cut from the ends. The railing is assembled on the ground, then raised and attached.

The clean-looking metal grid of this railing goes well with a deck that is painted to a high gloss. A stained, knot-free 2×8 sits on the railing. Check your local code for the maximum spacing allowed in the grid. Any such guideline is to keep children from falling through. Be wary of railings that have evenly-spaced horizontal pieces: Children may be tempted to climb them.

The bottom half of this railing is a solid wall, covered with grooved T1-11 siding and trimmed with rough-textured 2×4s and 2×6s. The top portion is made of 4×4s ripped to 3×3s. All parts are covered with opaque stain, which is nearly paint-like in its coverage but emphasizes the grain of the wood.

This railing uses lengths of standard metal fencing set between 4×4 posts. Distinctive in appearance, it is less expensive than having metal components custom made. The details at the tops of the posts are made entirely with cuts. The top is trimmed at a slight angle; and two grooves are cut below.

RAILING BASICS

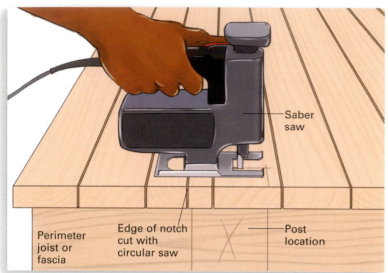

Use a circular saw and a saber saw to notch the old decking for each new post. Cut carefully so the post fits snugly in the notch.

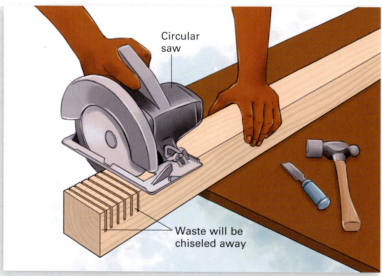

To notch a post, set a circular saw blade to a depth of 1¾ inches. Make a series of cuts spaced about ¼ inch apart, and chisel away the pieces.

A post that fits in the corner of a deck must be notched 1¾ inches along two adjacent sides. Start by cutting with a circular saw and finish with a chisel.

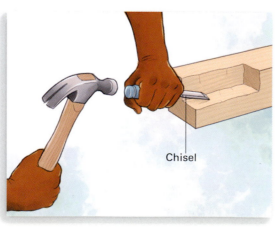

The fundamental steps for adding railings are the same as for building railings from scratch. If you want to modify an existing railing, use these instructions to install the necessary additional railing parts.

INSTALLING POSTS

Some decks use a "through-post" design: The posts supporting the deck continue upward as part of the railing. Through-posts aren't necessary on an existing deck unless you add a new elevated section and need support from the ground up. Railing modifications, however may require additional posts attached to the perimeter joists or fascia.

NOTCH THE DECKING: Place posts—as evenly spaced as possible—every 4 to 6 feet. Mark the side of the deck for each post. If the decking overhangs, cut a notch so that the post can rest flat against the perimeter joist or fascia. Use a circular saw to cut as much as possible, and use a saber saw to finish the cuts.

CUT AND NOTCH THE POSTS: Cut all the posts to the same length. This usually will be the height of the railing, less 1½ inches (if you install a 2× cap on top of the posts), plus the width of the perimeter joist and the thickness of the decking.

A post does not have to be notched unless it needs to match existing posts. Notch the lower section of each post: half its thickness and the length of the joist plus decking. If your plan requires a post in the corner, cut notches for both directions, *below left.*

INSTALL THE POSTS: Attach posts to the side of the deck with two lag screws or carriage bolts. Use bolts (bolts provide more strength) where you have a clear space on the inside of the joist. Drill holes while a helper uses a level to make sure the post is plumb.

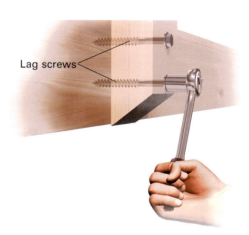

Attach the post by drilling pilot holes and driving lag screws, or drill wider holes and attach with carriage bolts.

After installing, check for plumb in both directions; if needed, loosen the screws or bolts and add a shim.

INSTALLING RAILS, CAP, AND BALUSTERS

Whenever possible, purchase rail and cap pieces long enough so you will not have to splice them. Most railing designs require a top and bottom rail, set either on edge or flat, and attached either to the interior or exterior post faces. In either installation, the top rail can be flush with the top of the posts or set a few inches below. Place the bottom rail about 3 inches above the deck surface.

Hold side-mounted rails in position and cut the joints so they are centered on a post. Attach the rails with two 3-inch decking screws or 16d galvanized nails in each side.

To install rails that will be attached between posts, hold each in place and mark for cutting. Use a helper when installing long pieces. Drill pilot holes and drive 10d galvanized nails or 2-inch decking screws.

INSTALL THE CAP: Use a straight 2×6 or 2×8 that is low in moisture content and free of large knots. Position each piece so it overhangs the post and the top rail, and mark for cutting. Attach with screws or nails driven into posts—and into the top rail if it is flush with the top of the post.

Outside corners can separate, warp, or split over time. To make the 45-degree cuts, use a power miter box or work carefully with a circular saw. Practice on scrap pieces for the correct angle. Attach the pieces by drilling pilot holes and driving screws. If you have a biscuit joiner, use it to make a tight joint, as shown at right.

GANG-CUT AND INSTALL BALUSTERS: Purchase ready-cut balusters, or make your own—2×2s make an attractive railing. You may want to angle-cut one or both ends on the outside faces. Determine where you will drive the fasteners. Set a group of balusters side by side, use a framing square to mark fastener positions and drill pilot holes.

Construct a jig to help maintain consistent spacing between the balusters. Install the first baluster plumb, then align the next few balusters. Check every five or six balusters to see that they are still plumb, and make adjustments if necessary.

If you must splice the rails, cut the ends at 45-degree angles and join the boards in the middle of a post.

Overlap cut at a 45° angle

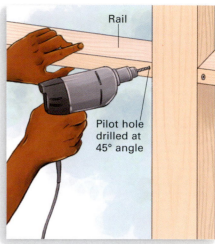

Rail

Pilot hole drilled at 45° angle

Work carefully when attaching flat-laid rails between posts. To avoid splintering, drill pilot holes at a 45-degree angle, then drive screws or nails.

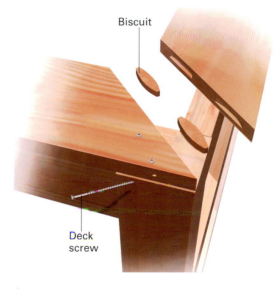

Biscuit

Deck screw

The mitered outside corner of a rail cap is often a trouble spot; it can come apart after a few years. Use a biscuit joiner to strengthen the joint. Drill a pilot hole and drive a screw to hold the pieces together.

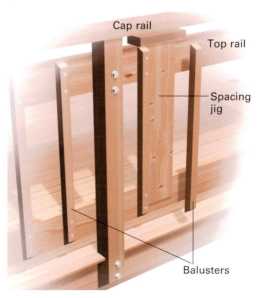

Cap rail

Top rail

Spacing jig

Balusters

A simple spacing jig keeps balusters evenly spaced. Place each baluster tightly against the jig, then fasten the baluster to the rails with nails or screws.

FOUR RAIL DESIGNS

A stylish railing is one of the most dramatic upgrades for a deck. These railings use add-on posts so they can be installed on an existing deck. All are fairly easy to build when you've mastered the basics described on pages 30-31.

Painting, sealing, and staining railings is difficult when they are assembled; there are just too many details to coat. Consider finishing your materials before building to save time, effort, and paint, sealant, or stain.

Note that unlikely materials often make attractive rails. Wire mesh, pipe, even acrylic plastic and canvas can—if well supported—be used as infill to replace balusters between posts.

WIRE RAILING

This design allows you to see through the railing, while providing a barrier. Order welded wire fabric from a metal fabricator and have it anodized. Or purchase less expensive "hog fence"— a heavy galvanized wire mesh—at a farm supply house. Spray paint it, or keep the galvanized look for a rustic effect.

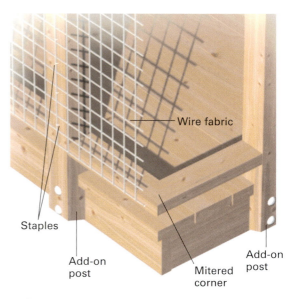

Attach posts, and install flat-laid 2×4 top and bottom rails. Attach the wire mesh to the posts and rails with 1½-inch galvanized fence staples. Attach a staple wherever a wire crosses a piece of wood. Cover the rail with a 2×6 or 2×8 cap.

LATTICE

Lattice provides privacy while letting the light shine through. Purchase heavy-duty, ¾-inch thick lattice. Lattice sheets are available in redwood or pressure-treated wood.

Lattice needs to be supported on all sides. Install flat-laid top and bottom rails between the posts. Cut pieces of 1×2; nail them to the

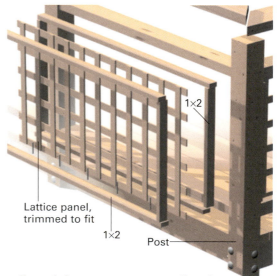

rails and the posts to act as nailers for the lattice. Cut the lattice to fit tightly between the rails and the posts. Attach the lattice by drilling pilot holes and driving 1¼-inch screws or 4d galvanized nails. Cover the ends of the lattice with narrow pieces of molding.

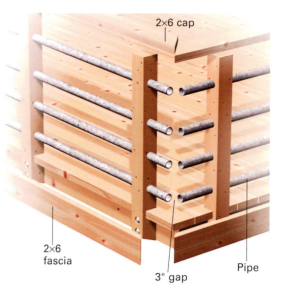

2×6 cap

2×6 fascia

3" gap

Pipe

PIPE RAIL

This railing is attractive, but it may violate building codes in your area because children can easily climb it. Use it on a low deck for decorative purposes only. Copper pipe will eventually turn a pleasant green. Stainless steel or chrome tubing will be distinctive.

Before you attach the posts, drill evenly spaced holes through them, sized so the pipes will fit snugly. Use a drill jig to ensure that

the holes are perfectly straight. Install the posts with lag screws or bolts, recessed so the heads will not get in the way of the 2×6 fascia. Attach the fascia, using miter joints at the corners. Measure and cut the pipes, slip them through the holes, and cover the top of the rail with a 2×6 or 2×8 cap.

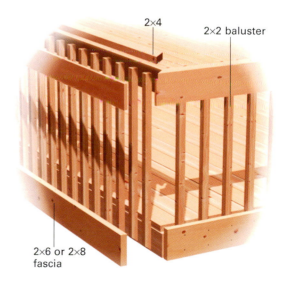

2×4

2×2 baluster

2×6 or 2×8 fascia

POSTLESS

This unusual design has no posts, giving it an airy feel. The narrow top cap is not practical for holding potted plants, but it emphasizes the upward-aspiring look. The decking must be cut flush to the edge of the outside joists or fascia so you don't have to cut hundreds of notches for the balusters.

With a helper, attach the balusters to the side of the deck. Use a level and a jig to make sure they are all plumb, and drive two screws through each of them. Make the top-rail-and-cap assembly

by screwing or nailing a 2×4 on top of two 1×6s. Keep the spacing correct by placing scrap 2×2 between the 1×6s before driving the screws or nails. This way, the assembly will fit over the balusters. Measure and cut the assembly. Tap it down with a hammer and a scrap of wood to keep from denting the 2×4. Use the baluster jig to space the balusters evenly. Drive a nail or screw through the 1×6 into each baluster. Cover the bottom of the balusters with a 2×6 or 2×8 fascia board.

STAIR BASICS

A deck stairway adds visual interest as well as utility. These pages contain instructions for building a standard stairway. On pages 36–37, we'll show you how to create larger stairways.

If you need to add a new stairway to an existing deck that already has a railing, remove the railing to the posts that are on either side of the stairway. Build the stairs first, then attach railings correctly sized for the stairway.

FIGURING RISE AND RUN

All steps in a stairway must be the same height and depth or they will feel awkward—and may be dangerous. Getting them consistent will require a bit of calculation; but first, some terminology.

RISE AND RUN: Rise refers to the height from one tread to the next. Run is the horizontal distance of each step—the depth of the tread, front to back. Total combined rise and run indicates the total vertical and horizontal distance traveled by the entire stairway.

Each step in a standard stairway has a rise of 6 to 8 inches and a run of 10 to 12 inches. There's a formula for the ideal relationship between the rise and run—twice the rise plus the run should be between 24 and 26 inches. The formula is the same whether you build stairs with either a standard or a more spacious dimension (see page 36).

ESTIMATING THE LANDING LOCATION: To calculate the rise on a level grade, measure from the deck surface to the ground and subtract 1 inch (the above-ground height of the landing). Measure out to your proposed landing site for the estimated run.

If the ground slopes, use the procedures shown in the illustration *below* to measure the rise and run.

Either way, dividing the rise by the riser height you want—for example, 7 inches (a standard rise)—will give you an idea of how many steps you need. Multiply that number by the tread depth you want (in this case, 10 to 12 inches) to estimate the total run. Mark the ground there for the end of your stairway.

FINAL ADJUSTMENTS: Adjust the height of the individual rise so the steps are even. For instance, if the total rise is 38 inches and you estimated five steps of about 7 inches, divide 38 (the total rise) by 5 (the number of steps) to get 7.6 inches. You'll have five steps that are about 7⅝ inches high. Adjust the individual runs (stay within the formula above) so the total run will put the bottom of the stairway where you want it.

BUILD THE LANDING PAD

The bottom of the stairway should rest on a firm, slightly sloped concrete or masonry surface about an inch above grade.

To make a concrete pad, dig out 8 inches of soil and install 2×8 forms staked with 2×4s. Add 4 inches of gravel, tamp it, lay in reinforcing mesh, and pour the concrete.

Carefully plan your stair layout. You may need fewer or more steps than you had anticipated; if so, measure again and refigure the dimensions.

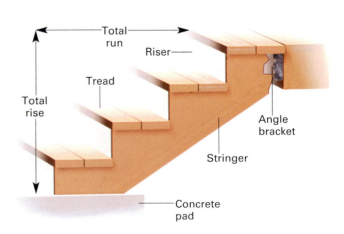

If your site is sloped, use straight boards and levels to help measure the rise and run and to locate the end of the stairs and the landing.

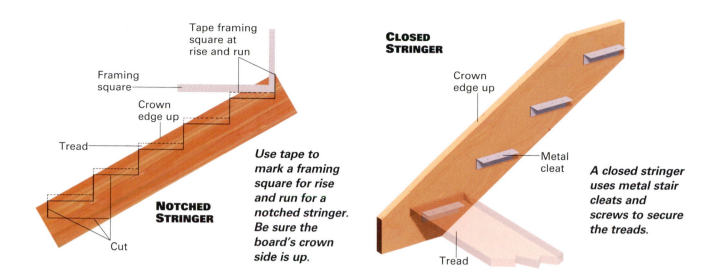

Tape framing square at rise and run

Framing square

Crown edge up

Tread

NOTCHED STRINGER

Cut

Use tape to mark a framing square for rise and run for a notched stringer. Be sure the board's crown side is up.

CLOSED STRINGER

Crown edge up

Metal cleat

Tread

A closed stringer uses metal stair cleats and screws to secure the treads.

Drag a straight board over the forms to level the concrete. Trowel it smooth.

You also can set bricks or pavers in sand (see page 22) or tamp gravel or stone inside timber edgings.

CONSTRUCT THE STAIRS

Take the rise and run calculations to a lumber supply retailer to compute the length of the stringers. Purchase straight, clear 2×12s.
MAKE THE STRINGERS: Mark the rise and run with tape on a framing square. With the 2×12 crown side up, draw light pencil lines. Start at the top, where the stringer will attach to the deck, and work downward. Mark the bottom step 1½ inches shorter than the others to allow for the thickness of the tread.

To make a notched stringer (with treads resting on the top of cut out notches), cut on your marks with a circular saw, stopping just short of the corners. Then finish with a hand saw. Apply sealer to all of the newly cut surfaces.

To make a closed stringer (with treads supported by cleats on the inside), cut the top and bottom only. At the lines, attach stair cleats with 1¼-inch decking screws driven through pilot holes.

ASSEMBLE THE STAIRS: Tack the stringers to the deck and mark the ground for post holes at the second or third step. Take the stringers down and dig holes at least 3 feet deep—or to the level specified by local codes. Attach the stringers to the deck joist or the framing you've added to provide firm support. Square the stringers, plumb and attach the posts, cut and attach the treads (notched around the posts, if necessary), and fill the holes with concrete.

Dig the post holes before you set the stringers, but install the posts after the stairway is framed, leaving enough post to trim to the correct height.

Post level

Concrete pad

Temporary brace

BUILDING LARGE STAIRS

Standard 3-foot-wide stairs with treads 11 inches deep are fine for taking out the garbage or other normal traffic. But if you want a pleasant place to sit and enjoy the view or if you want a more gracious access to the yard, consider more spacious steps.

These deep-tread stairways all have rise and run ratios that follow the "rule of 24-26." Twice the rise plus the run equals 24 to 26 inches.

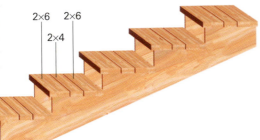

2×6   2×6
2×4

5½" RISE, 14½" RUN

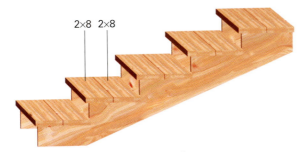

2×8 2×8

5" RISE, 14½" RUN

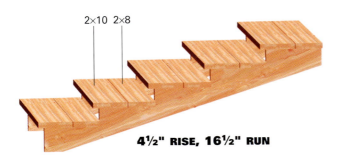

2×10 2×8

4½" RISE, 16½" RUN

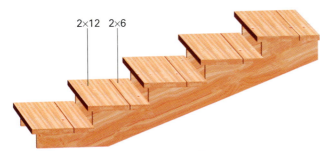

2×12   2×6

4½" RISE, 16¾" RUN

CALCULATING FOR COMFORT

As stair treads become longer, the rises should become shorter; otherwise, climbing them will be uncomfortable. Although the dimensions of most stairs—even those with larger treads—should comply with the 24-26 rise-to-run formula when possible (*see page 34*), some situations may not fit the "rule." These longer steps can still be comfortable to use.

LONG STEPS

To construct these stairs, use the same techniques as you would for a "formula" stairway, but adjust the placement of the lower end of the stairway to fit your site—even if such adjustment puts the stair dimensions outside the 24-26 formula. Construction methods are similar, except that the stringers will be longer and may need a support post on each side at the middle of the run.

FIGURING RISE AND RUN: First decide where you want the steps to end in the yard and then decide on a rise-run ratio. For instance, if you want to descend to a point that is 32 inches below the deck (total rise), and 70 inches away from the deck (total run), you could have five steps with rises of 6½ inches (5×6½=32) and runs of 14 inches (5×14=70). Of course, moving the landing pad a few inches in or out will simplify the calculations without affecting ease of use.

SUPPORTING THE STRINGERS: Use a framing square to mark 2×12s as you would for standard stringers, and cut them with a circular saw and a saber saw or handsaw (*see page 35*).

Stringers for wide stairs have a large "foot," so make sure the landing pad is wide enough to support all of it. The longer and more horizontal the stringer, the weaker it will be. As a general rule, if a stringer will not have support for more than 7 feet, support it in the middle—perhaps with a separate footing and post (in addition to the railing post near the bottom of the stairs).

TREAD COMBINATIONS: To get the width of tread you want, use any combination of boards that works. For instance, a 2×12 (11¼ inches wide) plus a 2×6 (5½ inches wide) with a ⅛-inch gap between them together form a 16⅞-inch-wide tread.

GENTLE LANDINGS

For a more gradual descent, build several landings—either in succession or separated by a short flight of steps. Landings extending more than 2 feet are no longer bound by the "rule of 24-26." Just be sure that all steps from one level to another—stairs or landings—are the same height, no more than 7½ inches.

In most cases, you will frame these landings separately—as you would a deck surface—but without an underlying beam. When calculating heights, remember to include the thickness of the decking.

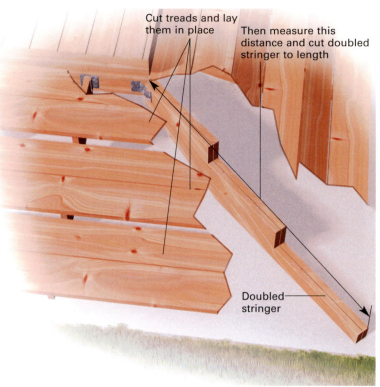

Cut treads and lay them in place

Then measure this distance and cut doubled stringer to length

Doubled stringer

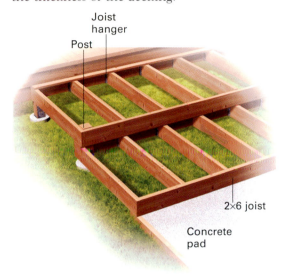

Joist hanger

Post

2×6 joist

Concrete pad

Frame descending landings as you would a deck surface, with joists, joist hangers, and posts with footings.

To frame stairs at a corner, first install a pad and stringers at the ends of each descent. Install a doubled stringer (two stringers nailed together, side by side) at an angle at the corner. It will be longer than the other stringers. Here's how to measure its length: First cut, miter, and temporarily set the treads in place, meeting in a mitered joint at the corner. Remove the treads from one side and measure the length that will support the bottom tread at the corner. Mark the stringers (the runs equal to the length of the miter), nail them together, then attach them to the deck frame.

HAND RAILS FOR SAFETY

A 2×6 or 2×8 is not comfortable to use as a stairway cap rail. Attached handrails are safer; you can buy ready-made materials or make your own.

To make your own, use the same stock as the rest of the railing. Rip a 2×3 from a 2×4 and round off the edges with a sanding block or a router with a roundover bit. Attach a 2×4 so it spans the inside edge of the stair rail posts a couple of inches below the rail cap. Cut 2×3 supports to hold the handrail, 2 inches out from the rail. That way, you'll have plenty of room to grab. Carefully drill pilot holes in the rail and the supports and attach them to the 2×4 with 3½-inch screws every 3 feet.

Purchase standard brass handrail hardware and rounded rail stock made for interior stairs. The rail stock is usually only available in pine or oak. Apply at least two coats of sealer to the wood (it's not designed for outdoor use) and secure the rail hardware to the post with extra-long screws.

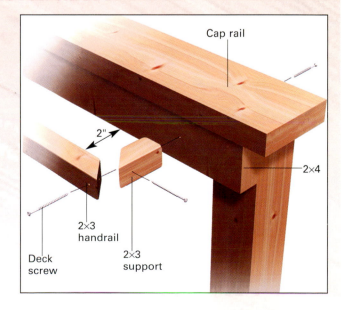

Cap rail

2"

2×4

2×3 handrail

2×3 support

Deck screw

ADDING A SKIRT

The underside of a deck can offer some difficult design challenges—large green-gray pressure-treated beams may be distracting, and the ground underneath may become muddy. Plantings of hedges or shrubs—chosen carefully so their mature height will not be higher than the deck—present an excellent solution.

You also can "skirt the issue." A well built wood skirt may be the most visible feature of your deck. It will enhance the style of your deck and enhance its utility by providing storage space. There are a number of different styles and material choices available for skirting a deck, and installing latticework and solid 1× stock are two of the easiest.

The skirt should visually cover up what is unsightly, but be sure the design allows air to circulate freely under the deck surface. If rainwater that seeps through the decking boards is not able to evaporate quickly, standing water can become stagnant and breed mosquitoes.

Provide a nailing surface for all parts of the skirt—top, bottom, and sides. If the below-deck posts are near the edges of the deck, you may be able to use them as part of the framing by running horizontal 2×4s between them.

If there is no easy way to attach the skirt, build a frame like the one shown, *below left*.

BUILDING SIMPLE FRAMING: Screw vertical 2×4s to the outside of the perimeter deck joists down to about 2 inches above grade. If you want to install lattice panels (*see opposite left*), place the 2×4s where two sheets of lattice will meet—the edges will need support. Next, make a top and bottom frame. On the same outside face of the deck joist, fasten a 2×4 between the vertical supports with half its width exposed below the joist. Attach the bottom frame, toenailed to the vertical supports, plumbing the vertical members as you go.

REINFORCING THE FRAMING: This simple framing assembly will not be very strong at the bottom. You'll need to reinforce it, especially if the deck is more than 2 feet from the ground and where people might bump into it. When you install the vertical 2×4s, place them next to a joist whenever possible. Joists on 16- and 24-inch centers should put the vertical supports at the lattice joints if you adjust the ends. Cut and miter (at 45 degrees) a 2×4 brace and screw it to the bottom of the vertical 2×4 and at the top to a joist or to the underside of the decking.

2×4 support

2×4 skirt framing

2×4 support

2×4

If the posts are spaced too far apart or are too short for framing, add framing below the deck for a surface to nail a skirt.

STOP THE GROWTH UNDER THE DECK

In some climates, almost no grass or weeds will grow in soil that is shaded by a deck. In climates where conditions encourage vegetation growth, many plants can spring up under—and even through—a deck.

First, dig up all the turf. Usually, you can just spread landscaping fabric over the area and shovel gravel on top to keep it in place.

Joist

Angled brace

2×4 skirt framing

Install an angled brace that is attached to a joist. The bottom of unbraced skirt framing will not be strong enough.

INSTALLING A LATTICE SKIRT

Lattice makes an ideal skirt material because it is decorative, easy to install, and provides plenty of ventilation. Use sheets of lattice that are at least ¾ inch thick, made of either redwood or pressure-treated lumber.

CUT AND ATTACH THE LATTICE PANELS: Smooth the ground beneath the deck so you don't have to cut the lattice to fit unusual contours. Cut the lattice so that all edges of the lattice panels will be supported by a framing member. Make sure the bottom of the lattice is about 1 inch above grade at all points (even pressure-treated lattice may rot if it sits in wet earth). Attach the lattice with 4d galvanized nails or 1¼-inch deck screws. If the lattice is brittle, drill pilot holes to prevent cracking it.

TRIM THE CORNERS AND SPLICES: Apply trim to all exposed edges at outside corners and where the ends of sheets come together. At a corner, cut one piece of 1×2 and one piece of 1×3 to cover the lattice; install with galvanized screws or nails. Position the 1×2 edge to butt up against the 1×3, so the corner appears to be balanced.

INSTALLING A SOLID SKIRT

Vertical 1×8s or 1×6s, spaced at ¾-inch intervals, will hide the space under the deck more than lattice. They form a solid skirt that does not allow as much ventilation.

ATTACH THE BOARDS: Starting at a corner, drill pilot holes and drive 2-inch deck screws to attach the boards to the top and bottom framing pieces. Use the thickness of a board as a spacer and check about every fifth board for plumb. You may want to trim the corners as described for the lattice skirt.

MAKE AN ACCESS DOOR

For storage or to provide access under the deck, make a door from three or four skirt boards. Tie the boards together with two horizontal nailers. Install flush hinges and an eyebolt latch.

To make a lattice door, cut a section of lattice to size and trim the edges with 1×4s on both sides. Drill pilot holes and drive 1⅝-inch screws every few inches in an alternating pattern. Attach the hinge to the face of the 1×4.

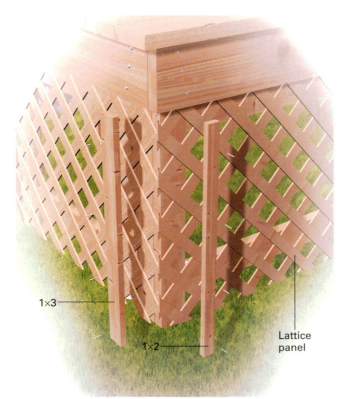

1×3

1×2

Lattice panel

Lattice skirting cuts easily and attaches quickly. If you don't like how exposed lattice edges look, trim the corners with 1×2 and 1×3 stock.

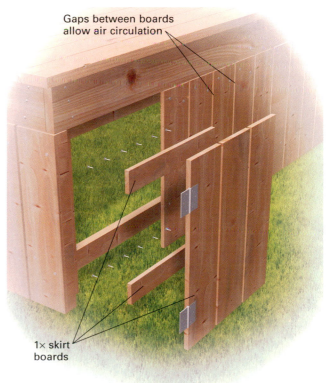

Gaps between boards allow air circulation

1× skirt boards

Attach solid vertical 1× boards leaving ¾-inch gaps between them for ventilation. Make an access door using the techniques shown on page 41.

A STORAGE HATCHWAY

Make this large storage bin to hold a hose, garden tools, or kids' toys. The drain holes in the bottom ensure that water will drain and items will stay dry. The joist through the center of this storage opening will not get in the way of most storage items.

I f your deck is at least 2 feet above the ground, you have plenty of potential storage space right below your feet. Make an access door to unlock that potential.

If all you need is periodic access to an under-the-deck hose bib, simply cut out and make the door. But for a usable compartment, build a storage box to keep equipment dry and within easy reach.

The compartment design at *left* is two joists wide (32 or 48 inches, depending on the spacing of the joists) with an uncut joist between them. This middle joist will not get in the way of most storage items. A pressure-treated plywood box will resist rotting; a grid of holes provides drainage for rain water.

FRAME THE DOOR OPENING

If the opening is larger than 3 feet by 4 feet, it'll take too much effort to lift the door. Use a framing square to draw lines on the decking for the center.

CUT THE OPENING: To make this plunge cut, set the blade at the thickness of the decking. Retract the blade guard and tilt the saw up. Rest the front edge of the base plate on the deck a few inches away from a corner of the opening. Place the blade just above the cut line, pull the trigger, and lower the blade slowly, holding the saw firmly so it does not skip away. When the blade has cut through and the saw is resting on the deck surface, stop the blade. Press a straight board against the side of the base plate and temporarily attach it to the deck. Using the board as a guide, cut each line with the circular saw, stopping short of the corners. Be careful not to nick adjacent boards. Finish the cuts with a saber saw or handsaw. Set the cut-out decking aside—you'll use it to make the door.

ATTACH FRAMING PIECES: The door will be heavy and it will get walked on, so build a strong support under it. Cut 2×8 (or wider) blocks to fit between the joists. Fasten them with pre-drilled screws or nails at an angle. The blocks will support the front and rear edges of the door, so make sure they're flush with the tops of the joists. Cut two pieces of 2×2 to fit between the 2×8s at the outside edges, and attach them to the sides of the joists.

MAKE AND SUPPORT THE BOX

If you just want access to the area under the deck, you can skip this part. If the box will be shallow and won't hold anything heavy, you

Circular saw

Cutting guide

Cut two lines in the decking along the inside edges of joists. A straight board tacked to the decking serves as a cutting guide.

can simply build it and attach it to the 2×8s and the joists. For a stronger box, first install a footing, post, and beam.

BUILD A SUPPORT: Use a plumb bob (or a chalk line) to locate and mark a spot on the ground directly beneath the center of the opening. Dig a hole at this spot and pour concrete for a footing. Depending on the distance between the ground and the deck, you may need to install a post anchor and post or a beam anchor for a beam that will rest directly on top of the footing. Make a beam several inches longer than the opening by laminating two 2×6s together. Attach it to the footing or post so it is level.

BUILD THE BOX: Build the box first, then slide it into position from below. Build it with ¾-inch pressure-treated or exterior-grade plywood, measured and cut to fit between the 2×8 blocking and the joists.

In the center of two of the sides, cut a notch 2 inches wide and a little deeper than the depth of your joist. When the box is assembled, the notches will allow the sides to fit around the center joist. Cut and assemble the four sides and attach them with 2-inch deck screws. Screw 2×2 support strips to the corners and at the bottom on all four sides.

Cut a bottom to fit, with cutouts at each corner to fit around the 2×2s. Drill a series of 1-inch holes for drainage. Drop the bottom plate in from the top of the box and screw through the 2×2 support strips to attach it.

Now slide the box into place from below the deck opening. It should fit snugly against the 2×2s. If you need to make up space, insert a flat-laid 2×4 between the bottom and the beam and drive screws into the 2×4 through the bottom of the box.

BUILD AND HINGE THE DOOR

Assemble the door on a flat surface. Lay out the pieces cut from the opening with the same spacing as the decking. Anchor the cutouts with scrap tacked to the deck and positioned snugly against the door pieces.

Cut two 2×6 or 2×8 braces—4 inches shorter than the door—and attach them perpendicularly with two 2½-inch coated screws at each joint. Use a drill and a saber saw to cut an oval hand hole about 2 inches by 4 inches.

Set the door in the opening. If necessary, cut one or two sides so the gap is even all around. Sand the edges of the door and the decking. Attach the door to the decking with two or three 1½×3-inch utility hinges.

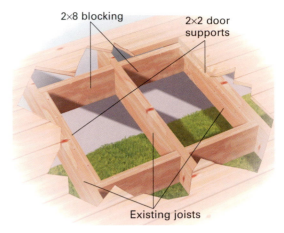

2×8 blocking · 2×2 door supports · Existing joists

Attach the framing pieces securely; they must support the hatch door as firmly as the rest of the deck's framing.

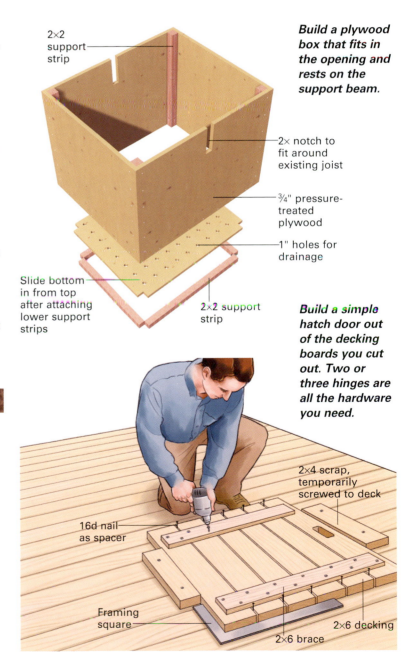

2×2 support strip · 2× notch to fit around existing joist · ¾" pressure-treated plywood · 1" holes for drainage · Slide bottom in from top after attaching lower support strips · 2×2 support strip

Build a plywood box that fits in the opening and rests on the support beam.

Build a simple hatch door out of the decking boards you cut out. Two or three hinges are all the hardware you need.

2×4 scrap, temporarily screwed to deck · 16d nail as spacer · Framing square · 2×6 brace · 2×6 decking

This arbor, combined with latticework screens, is an impressive entrance to an outdoor room. Behind it, elegant pillars support an overhead structure that cuts the glare of the sun and defines an area of the patio.

OVERHEADS

Whether you call it an arbor, pergola, lanai, or canopy, an overhead that shades and defines outdoor space will enhance your home with a minimum of materials and work. A large overhead can turn a deck or patio into an outdoor room, complete with "ceilings" and "walls." A small arbor between the yard and patio can be a pleasant focal point for your landscaping as well as a shady spot to sit and enjoy the outdoors.

The projects in this chapter have complete instructions, and you can modify them in several ways. A simple and airy structure with tall, thin posts and just a few top slats will look more solid with built-up posts and a layered "roof." Use off-the-rack lumber for the rafters, or cut them in ornate patterns.

If you want the overhead to provide shade, take the time to experiment to find the right amount of shade in the heat of a summer day and minimum amount when it's cooler. Of course, the closer the slats are spaced, the more shade they provide. But their direction matters too: If slats set on end run east to west, the sun will shine through them around noon, and they will provide shade in the morning and in the afternoon. Crisscross the slats in both directions to provide more constant shade. You can build the structure and then experiment with different slat configurations before attaching the pieces.

DO YOU NEED TO SINK POSTS BELOW THE FROST LINE?

If the posts for the overhead structure will be set in the ground, dig the post holes to extend below the frost line so they (and the overhead) won't rise and fall when the ground freezes and thaws.

Check with your local building department to find out how deep to dig for conditions in your climate.

GALLERY OF OVERHEADS

Additions to your outdoor landscape don't need to be attached to a deck to improve the landscape. Here, elements of a pergola over the deck extend to a freestanding arbor in the yard. A richly textured look develops from just a few types of materials and by sticking to the same style. Rafters made of 2×6s top the pergola, and support 4×4 top pieces on the arbor. When you have chosen the pattern, it will take only an hour or two with a saber saw to cut the winglike details on the rafter ends. Lattice can be purchased in sheets, so installation can be quick and easy.

Formal meets fanciful in this collage of geometric patterns. The 4×4 posts are trimmed with 1×2 stock. Making the intricate patterns between the posts—from 2×4s, 2×2s, and 1×2s—will take a good plan, a moderate amount of time and many accurate miter cuts.

An otherwise blank side of a house becomes lively with this simple overhead. The beefy 2×8 rafters, spanning only about 4 feet, are strong enough to support the swing. The overall effect is reminiscent of an old-fashioned front porch.

This elegant white-painted overhead blends with its stately surroundings. The posts are massive 6×6s attached to the deck. Trim pieces at its feet give them the look of classical pillars with pedestals. The beam is made of two 2×8s attached to both sides of the posts at the top; rafters are made of the same material. If you plan to paint an overhead, coat all the pieces with sealer and a coat of paint before installing them, then paint the whole structure again when in place. Latex exterior paint lasts well, but you may want the high shine of an oil-based enamel.

This easily installed, arched patio entrance graciously invites visitors. The four entry posts are 6×6s capped with mitered 2×4 pieces. Each curved arch is made of three pieces of 2×12. Rafters—made of 2×4s with long tapering cuts at the ends—provide lateral strength.

A large freestanding overhead provides a pleasant walkway through a casual stone patio. Posts made of 6×6s sunk deep in the ground support 2×6 beams, 2×4 rafters, and 2×2 top pieces. The arches are made of two pieces of 2×12 topped with 2×2s.

GEOMETRIC OVERHEAD

With squared ends and a strictly rectangular shape, this overhead is simple to build. Traditional homes call for a pressure-treated wood structure that is painted. For contemporary homes, use unfinished or stained redwood or cedar.

The rectangular grid of this overhead structure will cast a louver-like, slatted pattern on the deck below. If you want nearly square shadows, space the 2×6 rafters and the 1×3 top pieces 12 inches on center. For less shade and a lower material cost, space them at 16 or 24 inches on center.

START WITH THE LEDGER

Cut a 2×8 ledger and a 2×2 nailer to the length of the structure (as shown here, the ledger and nailer are each 10 feet long). The nailer helps support the 2×6 rafters so you don't have to use unattractive joist hangers. Attach the nailer flush with the bottom edge of the ledger using polyurethane glue and 6d galvanized box nails or 2-inch deck screws.

Next, cut the two 2×10 beams to the same length as the ledger. On both the ledger and the top of one of the beams, draw layout lines for rafters at 12, 16, or 24 inches on center, depending on the amount of shade you want. Be sure the beam is crown-side up.

Mark a level line on the house, at least 7 feet above the patio or deck (here, 8 feet). With helpers and steady ladders, lift the ledger and attach it to the house. (See instructions for installing the ledger to different surfaces on page 14.) This ledger does not need to be as strong as a deck ledger, but you'll need at least two fasteners every 16 inches to keep it from warping.

CLAD AND INSTALL THE POSTS

The 4×4 posts get their decorative interest from simple 1×4 and 1×8 cladding attached to opposite faces. Post installation is different for on-deck and in-ground installations.

ON A DECK: At the rear of the deck, measure from the decking to the top of the 2×2 nailer and cut the 4×4 posts to that length. Cut the 1×4 and 1×8 trim to the same length, and nail them to the posts with 6d galvanized casing nails, overlapping the 1×8s evenly.

On the front of the deck, mark the post locations. (Use the methods described on page 15 for squaring the locations of posts.) With a helper, raise each post, plumb it on two adjacent sides, and brace it temporarily with staked 1×4s. Anchor the posts to the decking by drilling angled pilot holes and driving 3-inch deck screws.

IN THE GROUND: Lay out the locations of the postholes as described above for on-deck

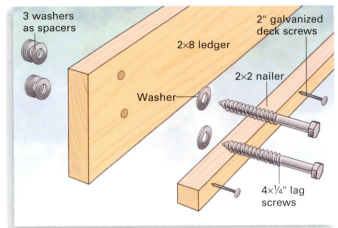

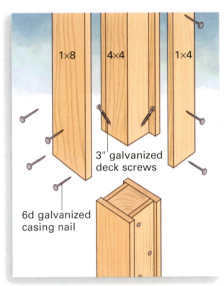

Adding 1× to a post bulks it up and covers knots and cracks. This treatment adds a crisp, professional-looking touch to the project.

Attach a 2×2 to the bottom edge of the ledger, then attach the ledger using this or any of the other methods shown on page 14.

post locations. Dig postholes to the depth required by local building codes (at least 3 feet deep), and shovel 4 inches of gravel in each one. Set the posts straight in the holes, leaving them uncut for now—you'll cut them to height later. Then, mark them about an inch above grade for positioning the bottom edge of the cladding. Remove each post, install the cladding, reposition the posts, and brace them securely and plumb on adjacent sides. Fill each hole with concrete, sloping the surface so water drains from it. Let the concrete cure for three days to a week.

With a helper, use a water level to mark the posts at the same height as the top of the 2×2 nailer. Transfer the cut line to all four faces of the post and cut the cladding and post with a circular saw and a handsaw.

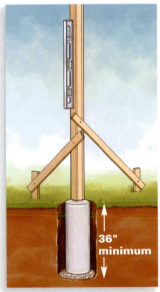

Set posts equidistant from the house (see page 15 for squaring corners) Then, brace and plumb them.

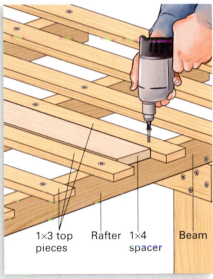

Deck screws provide enough holding power to attach beams to posts. Drive angled screws to hold rafters; one screw is enough for top pieces.

INSTALL THE "CEILING"

Three components—double beam, rafters, and top pieces—complete the project and provide its distinctive character.

INSTALL THE BEAMS: Determine how far you want the beams to extend beyond the posts, and mark and cut them to that size. With a helper on a ladder at one post and you at the other, set the first beam crown side up flush with the top of the post and centered on the length of the structure. Tack the beam in place with duplex nails (the type with two heads), then raise the second beam and tack it in place. Drill two holes centered on the posts and evenly spaced on beams, then fasten the beams with ⁵⁄₁₆×8 carriage bolts. Remove the duplex nails.

RAFTERS: Cut the rafters so they will overhang the front beam by 2 or 3 inches.

Set the rafters on the 2×2 nailer and attach them to the ledger and beams at the marks you made earlier. Use 2-inch decking screws driven at an angle into predrilled pilot holes. Then snap a chalk line at evenly spaced intervals across the tops of the rafters.

TOP PIECES: Cut the 1×3 top pieces to the same length as the beams. Using the chalk lines on the top of the rafters, position the top slats and attach them with a single 2½-inch galvanized or coated decking screw at each point the pieces intersect a rafter. Predrill the holes to avoid splitting the wood—especially at the ends.

DECK-SIDE ARBOR

This narrow overhead—with its cantilevered slatted roof—may provide just the shade you need in a particular spot. Encourage vines to climb up and over its top to increase the shade and add to its charm.

With its long, narrow profile, this overhead offers a number of practical and aesthetic solutions to difficult outdoor design problems. For example, use it to provide partial shade at a section of a deck or to hide a lounging area from the afternoon sun. Or use it to provide shade with a slim profile for an above-the-deck planter, keeping the plants cool and the soil from drying out.

Get the help of a helper or two to build it. Eight-foot ladders make the job easier and safer.

The 2×6 beams should span no more than 8 feet between posts. Make the 4×4 rafters 4 feet long. Pairs of rafters spaced 6 inches apart should be placed 30 to 36 inches between each pair.

INSTALLING THE POSTS

These posts are attached to a deck railing and anchored to the planting bed. To install this overhead next to a patio, dig holes at least 10 inches in diameter and at least 42 inches deep. Then set the posts in concrete *(see page 16)*. Cut the posts to the proper height after you've set them.

Attach the two posts for a deck installation to railing posts if possible, with one set in the

ground at an outside corner and one fastened to the house. Do not attach them to a rail that is loose. If you're in doubt about where to attach the posts, consult your local building department.

How you attach each post will depend on how your railing is put together. You will need to provide a flush nailing surface for the support post. Fastening a vertical 1×6 or 2×6 to the rail post will usually fill the space. Cut this spacer to fit between the top and bottom rail.

When the 1×6s or 2×6s are attached to the post, measure and cut 6×6 posts to the proper height. While a helper holds the post and plumbs it in both directions, drill pilot holes and drive 4×¼-inch lag screws through the top and bottom rail and into the post. Drive two or three screws through each rail. Offset the screws so they are not on the same grain line to lower the risk of cracking a rail. Attach the bottom of each post to the deck with at least two 4-inch angle brackets and screws.

FASTENING THE TOP FRAME

Use screws instead of nails to attach the upper frame so you won't shake the posts while you work. Once in place, the upper frame will

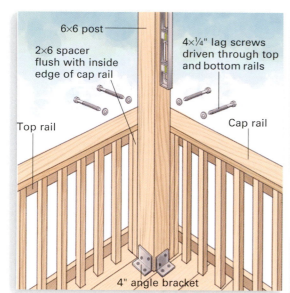

Choose a solid rail post—preferably one at a corner—and attach the new post to the railing top and bottom rails or directly to the railing post. You will probably need to add vertical 1×6s or 2×6s to fill the space between the rails and the new post to make the connection firm.

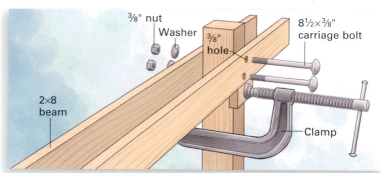

Clamped scraps of wood allow you to rest the beams while you work. Make a firm "sandwich" of post and beams with carriage bolts, nuts, and washers.

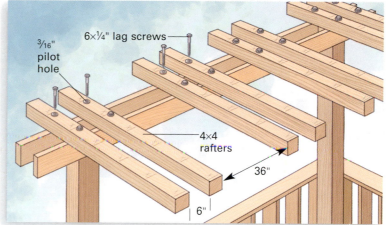

Before installing the rafters, mark them for the top slats and drill plumb pilot holes. When planning slat spacing, remember that you can't attach them over rafter screws.

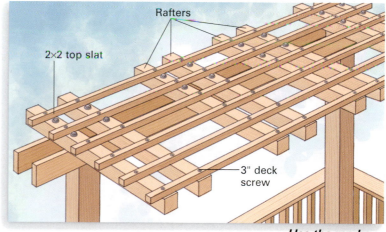

Use the marks on the rafters to fasten the slats evenly. Predrill the stock and attach the slats with screws.

strengthen the overall structure. Make sure the concrete has cured for three to seven days before attaching the upper frame of an overhead at the edge of a patio.

CUT AND ATTACH THE BEAMS: Cut two 2×8 beams to the length of the overhead, plus a foot or two of overhang on each end. Set them next to each other—crown edge up— and mark the positions for the 4×4 rafters.

Measure down 9 inches from the top of each post and clamp a piece of scrap on both sides. With a helper on a ladder at one post and you at the other, raise one beam and rest it on the scrap ledges. Center the beam between the posts and angle-drive a 2-inch deck screw at the top edge of the beam to hold it on the posts. Do the same with the other beam.

Drill holes—centered and evenly spaced, and countersunk for washers and nuts— and fasten the beams to the posts with two 8½×⅜-inch carriage bolts, washers and nuts. If you use longer bolts, cut the ends off after tightening the nuts.

THE RAFTERS: Cut all the 4×4 rafters to the same length—about 4 feet. Set them next to each other on a flat surface—crown side down—and mark the top edges where the 2×2 slats will be attached. Use a framing square and pencil to mark where screws will attach the rafters to the beams. Drill pilot holes carefully; if necessary, use a drill jig to ensure well-plumbed holes. Use a drill bit that is at least 6 inches long.

With a helper on another ladder working next to you, raise a rafter and lay it on the beams at the layout lines. Drill ³⁄₁₆-inch pilot holes through the pilot holes in the rafters and into the beams. Drive a 6×¼-inch lag screw (with a washer) into each joint.

TOP SLATS: Cut all the 2×2 slats to the proper length. In this installation, we have spaced them 8 inches on center. Space them closer together if you want more shade. Set the 2×2s on the layout lines, drill pilot holes, and drive a 3-inch deck screw into each hole.

ENTRANCE LANAI

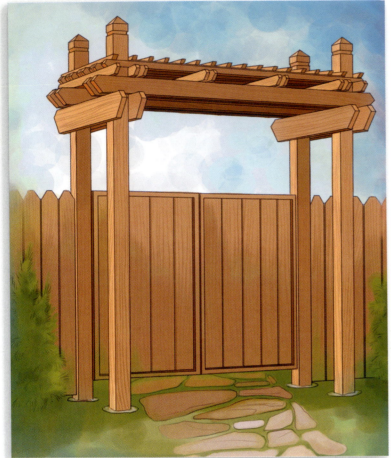

This fanciful design will add an Oriental flavor to your landscape, providing an unusual transition between the lawn and the patio or fenced deck location.

anai is a Hawaiian word meaning entrance or porch. This structure—with its five crisscrossed upper layers—will add a touch of the exotic to a fenced or unfenced deck or patio entrance.

The project may seem complicated at first, but all of the building steps are easy. Be sure to start with a square layout; use stakes and lines to mark the post locations. Building the rest of the structure is simply a matter of taking one layer at a time.

PREPARING THE POSTS

Because the lanai occupies relatively little ground space, you can lay it out easily with a full sheet of plywood as a guide or with stakes and lines. Use 4×4 posts longer than you need; you will cut them to the proper height later. For posts 11 feet above the ground, as shown at left, you will need 16-foot 4×4s.

LAY OUT AND PLACE POST HOLES: Lay out the site so the outside faces of the posts will form an 8×3 rectangle. If you use stakes and lines, measure the diagonals—when they're the same length, the layout is square. Dig the postholes at least 4 feet deep (or to the depth required by local codes), shovel in 4 inches of gravel, set the posts in, and brace them so they are all plumb and square to each other (see page 53 for examples of bracing techniques). Fill the holes with concrete, sloping the top to allow for drainage. Let the concrete cure for three days to a week.

If you want to finish the project quickly, you can pour the concrete after the entire structure is built—but make sure the posts are well braced.

CUT AND CAP THE POSTS: Working with a helper on two tall stepladders, use a water level or carpenter's level attached to a straight board to mark the posts for cutting (*see page 16*). Do not measure each post height from the ground—even a small discrepancy will cause big problems later.

Transfer the marks to all faces of each post with a square, then cut them with a circular saw. Attach decorative post caps to the tops of the posts: Drill pilot holes, apply a thin layer of polyurethane glue to the top of each post, then drive four casing nails.

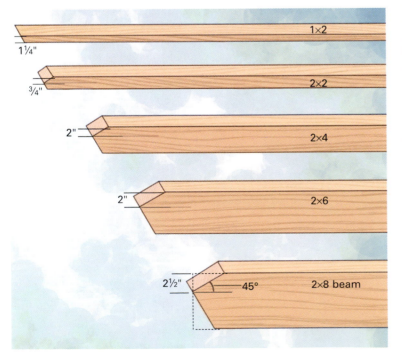

1¼"   1×2

¾"   2×2

2"   2×4

2"   2×6

2½"   45°   2×8 beam

Cut the pieces as shown at left to give the overhead structure a pleasant form. Use a triangular speed square or a combination square to mark 45-degree angles that converge at a point about one third of the way under the top edge.

BUILDING THE UPPER LEVELS

In this lanai, four 2×8 beams support four layers of lumber in decreasing sizes: 2×6s, 2×4s, 2×2s, and 1×2s.

CUT AND INSTALL THE BEAMS: Cut a 2×8 beam to the depth of the entrance (3 feet in this design) plus 24 inches so it overhangs the posts by 12 inches on each side. To make the end cuts shown, *opposite*, mark a point on the end of the beam 2½ inches from the top. At that point, mark a line parallel to the top edge. Use a small square to mark 45-degree lines that meets at the point, then cut on the lines. Using the first beam as a template, mark and cut the other three. You can also use any of the other beam-end styles shown at right.

Working with a helper, clamp scrap ledges 40 inches below the top of the posts. Rest the beams on the scraps as you attach them with carriage bolts into predrilled holes.

PLAN THE OVERHEAD ARRANGEMENT:
The number of upper pieces depends on the size of the lanai, the look you want, and the amount of shade you need. Sketch the configuration on graph paper, with each square equal to 1 inch. Your lanai may use fewer or more roof members than are shown here. Note that the 2×6s, 2×4s, and 2×2s are arranged in pairs, while the 1×2s are evenly spaced.

CUT THE UPPER PIECES: Cut the 2×6s, 2×4s, and 2×2s in the same way as the beams. Measure the 2×6s so they overhang the beams by 16 inches on each side, then cut each succeeding layer 8 inches shorter than the previous one. Note that the 1×2s have only a single 45-degree cut.

INSTALL THE "ROOF" LAYERS: Fastening the final layer is fairly easy because you can lay all the stock for each layer on top of the previous layers. Remember to draw layout lines on the top edges of the boards before installing them.

Start with the four 2×6s. Set them next to each other, crown side up, and mark the top edges to show the positions of the 2×4s in the next layer. Set the 2×6s in place next to the posts, overhanging an equal distance on either side. Attach them with two 3-inch deck screws at each joint.

Using the same procedures, mark and install the succeeding roof layers. Remember to take the post positions into consideration when marking the tops of one course for the next. Attach the 2×4s to posts where possible; drill angled pilot holes and drive screws. Attach the 2×2s by drilling pilot holes and driving 3-inch screws down into the 2×4s; use 2-inch screws for the 1×2s.

For a more decorative touch, cut the ends of the beams and other upper members in patterns like these. Use a circular saw for straight cuts, a router for chamfered edges, and a saber saw for curves. When you have cut one piece to your satisfaction, use it as a template for the others.

You can find a variety of post caps at your home center or deck yard. Attach them by drilling pilot holes, applying polyurethane glue, and driving casing nails.

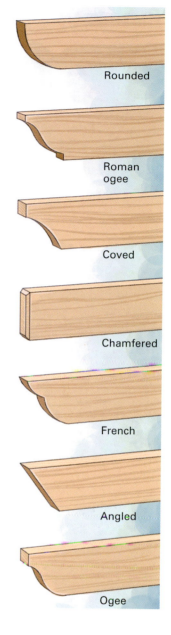

Rounded

Roman ogee

Coved

Chamfered

French

Angled

Ogee

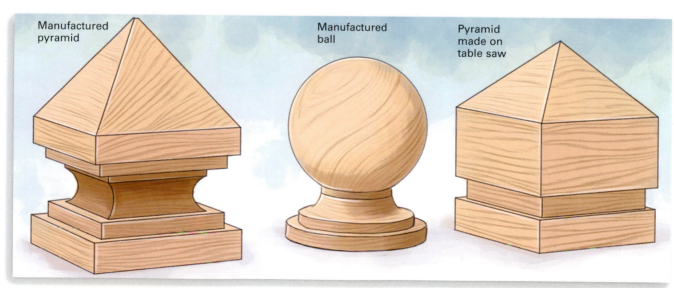

Manufactured pyramid

Manufactured ball

Pyramid made on table saw

ARCHED ARBOR

Wonderfully adaptable to a variety of landscape designs, this arbor is also surprisingly easy to build. To cut the curves of the rafters, rent a professional-grade saber saw.

A graceful curve can make the difference between a plain-looking structure and a focal point for your yard.

Build this arbor to provide an arched transition from your deck or patio to the garden or planting beds in other areas of your yard. The design will stand alone without the benches, but incorporate them if you want to make this a spot for relaxation or quiet conversation. Plant vines or climbers to help define the space as a private retreat.

SET AND BRACE THE POSTS

In this design, the arbor forms a 92×60-inch rectangle. You can change these dimensions to suit your site. For small layouts, use a sheet of plywood to mark the posthole locations—spaced so the pairs of the 4×4 posts will be 14 inches apart at the outside edges. Lay out larger sites with batter boards (*see page 15*).

Dig holes at least 3 feet deep (or to the depth required by local building codes) and shovel in 4 inches of gravel. Set the posts in the holes; you will cut them to the proper height later. Brace the posts plumb in both directions and fill the holes with concrete. Slope the top for drainage and let the concrete cure for three days to a week.

MAKING THE BENCHES

This simple bench design consists of 2×4 seat slats resting on 2×6 framing. You may want to incorporate bench design ideas shown on pages 66-71.

For each bench, cut two 2×6 rails to span the outside edges of the posts. Mark the posts about 15 inches from the ground. Level the rails with a carpenter's or line level and predrill ⅜-inch holes below the marks. Fasten the rails to the posts with ⅜×5-inch carriage bolts. Counterbore the interior post edges for washers and nuts.

Cut 2×6 side rails to fill in between the front and back rails and attach them with 3-inch decking screws.

Next come the seat slats. Cut them from 2×4s and make them 3 inches longer than the front-to-back width of the 2×6 framing. Set the slats on the frame and adjust the spacing so you come out even and don't have to rip-cut a 2×4. Temporarily nail or screw a piece of 2×2 to the top edge of the front and back rails and use it as a guide to keep all the pieces overhanging each edge by 1½ inches. Attach the 2×4s by driving two 3-inch deck screws into each joint. Sand the top and bottom edges thoroughly to prevent splinters.

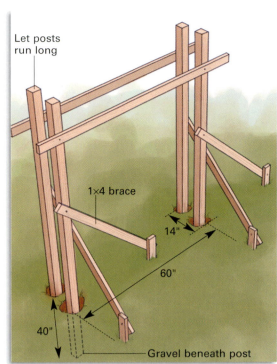

Let posts run long

1×4 brace

14"

60"

40"

Gravel beneath post

Use 1×4 bracing to hold the eight posts securely in place so they are square to each other, plumb, and the correct distances apart.

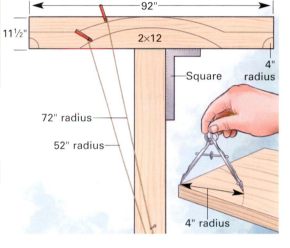

3" deck screws

2×6

2×4

2×6

4×4 post

Temporary 2×2 guide

Cut and lay all the 2×4 bench slats on the 2×6 framing, and adjust the spacing so a 2×4 butts against the posts at both ends. Use a tacked 2×2 to maintain an even overhang as you attach the bench slats.

92"

11½"

2×12

Square

4" radius

72" radius

52" radius

4" radius

Using a string compass, you can mark symmetrical curves. Stretch the string consistently and hold the pencil firmly at a consistent angle as you draw. Make corner cutouts with a compass or jar lid of the desired diameter.

MAKE THE CURVED RAFTERS

Cut two of the 2×12 rafters to length—92 inches for this design. Lay them on a flat surface to form a T, with the vertical piece centered on the horizontal piece.

Make a string-and-pencil compass—partially drive a screw in the center of the vertical piece, 72 inches down from the top of the horizontal board. Tie one end of mason's line (it doesn't stretch as much as string) to the nail and the other end to a pencil so the pencil touches the top of the horizontal piece when the line is taut. Hold the pencil at a consistent angle and draw an arc on the horizontal piece.

Now, measure 4 inches from the top of the horizontal board and another 52 inches from that point. Remove the screw, and again, partially drive it in—this time at the 52-inch mark. Draw an arc with the 52-inch radius.

Use a compass or a jar lid to draw small arcs on the bottom outside corners of the rafter. Cut the straight lines with a circular saw, then use a saber saw to cut the curves. Use a professional-quality saber saw—homeowner models usually cut slowly and wobble, producing uneven cuts. Use the first rafter as a template to mark the remaining rafters and cut them also. Sand all the edges.

If you size the rafters differently, make sure they are at least 4 inches thick.

RAFTERS AND SLATS

Mark and cut one corner post at 7 feet. Then mark the other corner posts at 7 feet and use a level on a straight board to mark and cut the remaining posts. Next mark the posts at the point you want to attach the rafters. Clamp scrap at these marks on both sides of the posts. With a helper set one rafter on the scrap ledges and adjust it so it overhangs equally on either side. Tack it temporarily and then raise and tack the second rafter. Drill ⅜-inch holes centered on the posts and spaced evenly from the rafter edges. Attach the rafters with ⅜×6½-inch carriage bolts. Using the same methods, install the rafters on the other side of the arbor. (Special-order the bolts or use 7-inch bolts and cut them after installing the rafters.)

Cut the 2×2s to a length that overhangs the rafters 3 inches on either side. Using a 2×2 as a spacer, fasten the slats with 3-inch deck screws in predrilled holes. When you are several pieces from the end, you may have to adjust the spacing so the slats come out even.

A classic picket fence is fun to build and is a lovely setting for climbing plants. Two coats of exterior paint will give any color a rich depth and sufficient protection from the elements.

FENCES AND WALLS

Fences and walls can be a beautiful addition to a deck or patio, connecting it to the larger landscape and defining areas of lounging, gardening, and play.

They also can be problem solvers. Perhaps you've wanted a larger patio for some time, but your backyard includes a steep slope—right where you want the patio. You can grade the slope, hold it back with a retaining wall, and expand your patio onto the level area.

Or maybe there's usable space near your deck or patio, marred only by a straight-on view of the neighbor's garage or compost heap. Block the view with a fence, then enlarge your outdoor living space. Or perhaps your deck or patio is too large; a fence or wall can divide it into smaller, less imposing spaces.

Many local building codes have setback requirements for how far away from the property line you may put a fence or other structure, how tall a fence can be, even which styles are permitted. Check with your local building department before you start building.

Masonry walls require hard work and a fair amount of skill. Such a project is often better left to professionals. But with only a bit of do-it-yourself experience, you can build an attractive dry-laid masonry wall (see pages 62–63), a retaining wall with interlocking blocks (see page 64), or a timber wall that will hold back a small mountain of soil (see pages 64–65).

GALLERY OF FENCES AND WALLS

A solid-paneled fence provides maximum security and protection from wind. Here, 6×6 posts with decorative caps anchor a 5-foot solid fence with 2 feet of latticework at the top. The fencing is made of vertical tongue-and-groove 1×6s set between horizontal 4×4 top and bottom rails. The lattice panels are made of molded plastic that are easy to maintain. The fence is painted in two tones of glossy, oil-based enamel for a polished look.

A stone retaining wall suits this free-form landscape that blends the pool, plantings, and brick walkways. Although construction of a wall this large is a project better left to the professionals, a shorter version would be well within the scope of a do-it-yourselfer (see pages 62–63).

A stucco-coated base wall creates a background that accents the profuse plantings. Both the wall and the weathered stake gate create an effect that is reminiscent of a Southwestern courtyard.

A cut stone wall forms a large planter, providing a natural setting for a small statue. These stones are set in mortar. For a lower planter in a less formal setting, lay dry-set stones around a galvanized planting base.

A high brick wall is ideal for congested neighborhoods where privacy and noise baffling are important. A large structure like this should be installed by a professional mason.

Fences and large planters made of redwood that have been allowed to gray provide a neutral background that allows the bright colors of the flowers to dominate.

BASIC FENCE BUILDING

M ost fences are made with 4×4 posts sunk into the ground, with two or three horizontal 2×4 rails that support vertical or horizontal boards or panels (often called the infill). Use materials that will resist rotting: pressure-treated lumber or naturally resistant species such as redwood, cedar, or cypress. Even if painted, untreated pine and fir will not outlast pressure-treated pine.

LAYING OUT AND SETTING POSTS

Estimate the location of the ends or corners of the fence and drive stakes into the ground to mark them. Construct batter boards from two pointed 2×4 legs and a crossbar (all pieces should be 2 feet or longer). Pound them into the ground about 2 feet beyond the corners and ends.

ESTABLISH SQUARE CORNERS: Tack a nail on each crossbar and stretch mason's lines from batter board to batter board.

Establish fence lines that conform to local setback requirements. Use batter boards and mason's line to lay out straight lines and square corners. One person can shift the post and check for plumb in both directions with an inexpensive post level. Post spacing will vary with fence design and materials used.

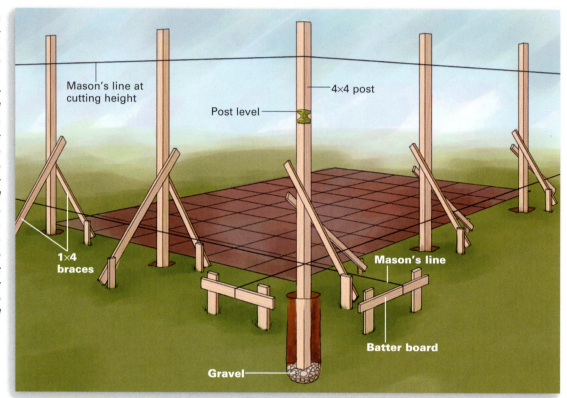

When the posts are set and cut, measure for inside rails. Use scrap wood to keep the bottom rail about 6 inches above the ground until you toenail it with 8d galvanized nails or use 2½-inch deck screws.

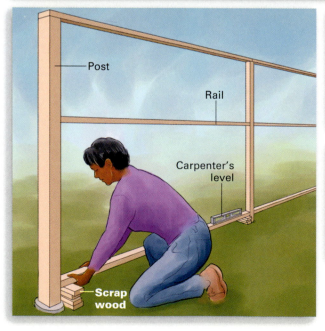

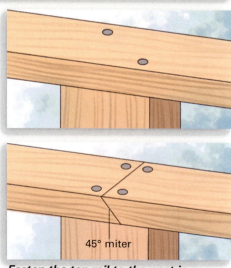

Fasten the top rail to the post in a diagonal pattern to avoid splitting the post. Miter adjoining pieces.

STEPPED FENCE

Infill set plumb

Level rails

Install plumb posts on a sloped site as you would on a level site. For a stepped fence (left), attach level rails and then cut the posts. For a sloped fence (right), cut the posts and install the rails so they follow the slope of the ground. Install the infill plumb in both cases.

SLOPED FENCE

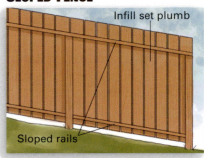

Infill set plumb

Sloped rails

Toenailed joint

Rail hanger

Toenailing galvanized nails or screws won't show as much, but rail hangers and other fence hardware make stronger rail joints.

Square the corners with the 3-4-5 method (*see page 15*). Use a plumb bob to mark the ground for the position of the posts.

MARK INTERIOR POST LOCATIONS: Many fences have posts spaced 8 feet apart; your site and design may require different spacing. Lumber is sold in even-numbered increments, so space the posts in even multiples of feet to avoid wasting material.

If you use factory-made panels, place the posts precisely. Measure carefully or lay the panels on the ground to determine post locations. (If you're using prefabricated panels, you can mark and dig post holes as you go. This method involves setting a post, holding a panel in place, marking the next post hole location and digging it.)

DIG THE HOLES: Dig holes at least half as deep as the exposed height of the post. Use a clamshell digger or rent a power auger. Some fence or landscaping companies will dig postholes for a reasonable price.

PLUMB THE POSTS: Shovel 4 inches of gravel into the holes so the post bottom does not sit in wet soil. Set each post in place, strap a post level to it, and hold it securely with two braces and stakes.

SET THE POSTS: Some builders prefer to fill the holes with concrete; others prefer tamped sand or soil. Check with local builders or your building department to see which method works best for local conditions.

■ **IN CONCRETE:** Mix concrete in a wheelbarrow with a mason's hoe or a gardener's hoe. Shovel the concrete into the hole. Poke a steel rod into the concrete and move it up and down at several points to remove air bubbles. Mound the concrete an inch or two above grade, and slope it down and away from the post.

■ **IN TAMPED SOIL:** Shovel in a foot or so of soil, then tamp it firm with a 2×2 or metal rod. Take the time to tamp firmly. Repeat until it is filled to the top. Mound the soil up and tamp it firmly with a 4×4 so rainwater will run away from the posts.

FRAMING THE INFILL

Before adding rails and infill (*see pages 60–61* for options), cut the posts. Stretch a taut line from one end or corner post to the other.

If the ground is fairly level, or if you want the fence to follow the slope, attach the line at both ends the same height from the ground (you can use a water level to make sure the height is the same). Mark all the posts at the line and cut them with a circular saw.

If you want a fence that steps down (*above left*), use the same method to establish heights, but install fence sections that are plumb, then cut the posts.

INSTALL RAILS: Cut 2×4 rails to span the outside faces of the posts or to fit snugly between them. For inside rails, hold the rail in place and mark it. Attach the rails with rail hangers, or predrill pilot holes for galvanized nails or screws.

CUT AND ATTACH INFILL: Cut the infill lumber at the same time, and make a spacing jig to speed installation. If the infill stock is wider than 2 inches, attach it with two nails or screws at each joint.

ADD A KICK BOARD: To keep the dog in the yard, add a kick board at the bottom—extending almost to the ground. If your pet likes to dig under the fence, install a pressure-treated board in a trench dug several inches into the ground.

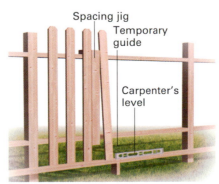

Spacing jig
Temporary guide
Carpenter's level

A spacing jig and a level guide board at the bottom allow you to install pickets quickly and accurately.

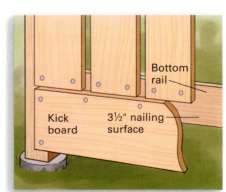

Bottom rail
Kick board
3½" nailing surface

To install a kick board, position the bottom rail on end so you have 3½ inches of nailing surface.

FENCE DESIGNS

When the posts and rails are installed, completing the fence is relatively quick and easy. Add some architectural detail to your fence—a little extra work and a small amount of money for materials can make the difference between a dull fence and an eye-grabber.

CHOOSING A DESIGN

When you find a design you like, it's usually simple a matter to figure out how to construct it. Here are four common designs.

POINTS ON EVERY OTHER BOARD: Alternating board widths adds a bit of visual interest; to liven the design more, point the end of every other board. Cut one, then use it as a template for marking the others. With a power miter box or a radial arm saw, you can cut points on four or five boards at a time.

ALTERNATING SIDES: Attach the infill on one side, using a piece of infill stock as a spacer so you leave off every other picket. Then do the same on the other side, positioning the pickets so they alternate with the spaces on the first side. This design provides nearly complete privacy without being too wall-like.

BASKET WEAVE: Center a 2×2 on the inside face of each post fastened with 4d galvanized nails or 2-inch deck screws. Then, install vertical 2×2s every 2 to 3 feet between the posts.

Purchase 1×6s or 1×8s that are not completely dry. Weave one of them between the 2×2s. Slide it even with the nailer on one post then mark and cut it to fit at the other end. Use this length to mark the remaining infill pieces and weave them from alternating sides.

ALTERNATING HIGH-LOW: Making every other board higher is another variation for vertical pickets. In the example shown, a 1×3 is used to space the pickets for a half-open look.

FACTORY-MADE PANELS

Visit a home center or a lumberyard that specializes in outdoor wood products—you may find ready-made fence panels that cost less than some individual pieces of lumber.

Some panel manufacturers, however, don't use the highest quality wood. Check for knots, cracks, and other defects—they are sure to become worse. Make sure the lumber that the panels are made of is the same thickness throughout and will hold up to the conditions of your climate. Paint them or give

POINTS EVERY OTHER BOARD

BASKET WEAVE

ALTERNATING SIDES

ALTERNATING HIGH-LOW

them a couple coats of sealer. If the boards are fastened flimsily (often with staples), add screws to reinforce the joints.

You can turn flimsy construction into an asset—dress up a plain panel by shuffling infill members around, or remove every other board and cut a design in the top of the panel. Or, drill a hole near the top of every other board. Any alteration you make will reduce the strength of the panel, so compensate by installing extra fasteners. An alternative is to purchase panels of two designs and mix the infill to alternate the two styles.

LATTICE FENCING

Lattice fencing lets a soft, filtered light shine through and makes a great support for climbing vines. Paint or stain the lattice before installing it: Lay it on scrap pieces of wood that have been set on a drop cloth, and use a paint sprayer.

Plan the framing so you can fit full widths of lattice panels on it; otherwise, you will waste material. Lattice should have a nailing surface every 3 feet or less, or it may warp. Install rails set on edge so you will have plenty of nailing surface.

Attach the lattice by driving 4d galvanized nails or 1¼-inch deck screws every 6 inches. Cover the edges with trim. Use 1×2s for the trim, or use leftover pieces of lattice.

CUT SCALLOPS ON FENCE SECTIONS

To cut a scallop, first install the pickets with the bottom ends straight (use a tight, level mason's line or tack a level guide board to the posts). Cut to height only those pickets that will be at the peaks of the scallops; these can be the pickets attached to the posts if the posts are evenly spaced.

Tape a length of soft, unkinked rope to two peak pickets. Stand back and see whether it is the shape you want, and adjust if necessary. Mark each picket with a pencil running along the rope. Cut the pickets with a saber saw, and give the cut ends a quick sanding to prevent splinters.

Rail cap
Lattice stock cut for trim
Post
Lattice
1×2 nailer
Rail

Design the framing so it can support the lattice every few feet. Install a rail cap on top and trim the sides with pieces of lattice.

Ready-made fence panels can be inexpensive as well as time-saving. Check out the material and construction quality to make sure the panels will last. Sometimes it's worth buying an extra panel for pieces to replace damaged pickets.

RETAINING WALLS

Retaining walls can cut into slopes, freeing space otherwise unsuitable for a deck or patio surface. A dry-laid stone wall (one laid without mortar) is strong enough to hold back soil and can be an attractive feature of a patio area. Build walls no higher than 4 feet; any dry-laid stone wall taller than that will be unstable.

DRY STONE WALL

Building a wall with no mortar holding the pieces together does not require masonry skills, but it does require patience and a strong back. You will spend most of your time trying one stone and then another to create a stable fit.

All the projects on the following four pages involve the kind of heavy physical labor that can strain your lower back. Enlist helpers or work only a couple of hours a day and let the job stretch out over several weekends.

BUYING THE STONE: Use stones that are more flat than round; thick flagstones are ideal for a low wall. A stone supplier can help you estimate how many you will need. Have the stones dropped off as close to the job site as possible.

EXCAVATE AND PROVIDE DRAINAGE: The job of grading back a slope for a patio or deck expansion probably should be left to a contractor—especially if the area is large. When the excavation is complete, stretch mason's lines between stakes to mark the ground for a trench twice as wide as the wall will be thick.

Remove all turf and any large roots, and dig to a depth of about 6 inches. If you build against a slope where rainwater runs off, use perforated drainpipe and landscaping fabric as shown in the illustration *below*. Shovel in gravel to nearly fill the trench, and tamp it firm with a hand tamper.

LAY THE FIRST COURSE: Sort the stones into several piles so you can easily find small, medium, and large stones. Use large flat stones for the base, which will be slightly wider than the top. Set stones on the gravel in two parallel rows. Twist and shift each one, and perhaps remove or add gravel, so it sits solidly and does not wobble. You may need to fill in the middle with small stones.

To keep the weight of water runoff from destroying your retaining wall, install a drainage system. Lay perforated drainpipe in gravel so it can carry water away to a dry well or another area that will soak up the runoff. Lay gravel, then landscaping fabric. As you build upward, fill the area behind the wall with gravel, and finish off the top with soil and sod or plantings.

Soil backfill

Landscaping fabric

Soil   Gravel

Perforated plastic drainpipe

Paver

BATTER THE FACE: A retaining wall must be battered—its face should slope toward the soil that it will hold back. Make a batter guide like the one shown at right, and use it periodically to check that the wall is properly sloped.

KEEP ON STACKING: Stack two or three rows of large flat stones at the ends of the wall, then fill in the middle. Always set one stone on top of where two meet so that the joints are offset. Use small stones to fill in spaces and to stabilize larger stones. About every 8 square feet, lay a very large bonding stone so it rests on the front and back rows and ties them together. Save particularly good-looking and large stones for the top row.

For additional strength, set the top layer of stones in a bed of mortar.

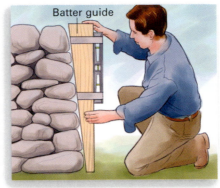

Batter guide

Make a batter guide from a board cut to the height of the wall, then cut at an angle along its length so that it is tapered 1 inch for every 2 feet of rise. Tape a level to its straight side, and use it to check the wall as you build. When the bubble is centered, the angle is correct.

Because they are flat and of fairly consistent thickness, flagstones are easy to dry-lay. They are ideal for low walls like this.

STUCCOING A CONCRETE OR MASONRY WALL

Flat trowel

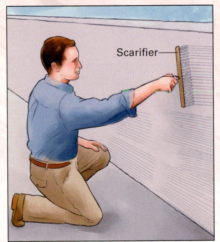

Scarifier

Flat trowel

If a solid but homely block wall borders your patio area, dress it up with stucco, a thin coating of special concrete mix you can buy in bags.

First, paint the wall with a latex concrete bonding agent. Mix a bag of stucco mix in a wheelbarrow, adding water until it reaches a toothpaste-like consistency.

Scoop the mix onto a flat trowel using a board or mason's trowel. Starting at the top, apply the stucco firmly. Smooth it out until it is about

³⁄₈ inch thick. Before it dries, scratch the surface with a scarifying tool, or a 12-inch 1×4 with about 16 evenly spaced nails protruding through it. Score it horizontally about ¼ inch deep—not quite all the way to the wall surface. Let the first "scratch" coat dry for two days. Keep it from drying too quickly with a covering of plastic, or spray it with a fine mist every few hours.

Apply a ³⁄₈-inch finish coat with the same trowel. To achieve a

consistent-looking finish, develop a troweling technique and stick with it—perhaps long, sweeping strokes, short strokes in several directions, or arcing strokes. Use a whisk broom to add some final swirls. Allow the second coat to dry slowly, as you did the first coat. Be sure it is completely dry before you apply paint. Select a paint made for concrete surfaces and rated to withstand the range of weather conditions common to your area.

RETAINING WALLS
continued

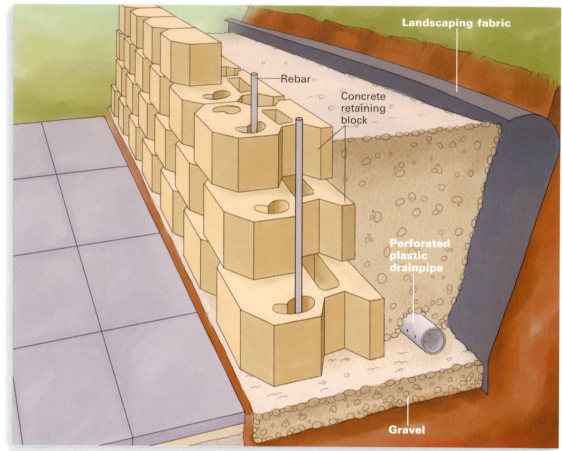

When the excavating is finished and you have a level trench, laying the concrete retaining blocks is easy. Rebar helps provide lateral strength. Walls more than 2 feet tall should be battered (see pages 62–63).

Labels on illustration: Landscaping fabric · Rebar · Concrete retaining block · Perforated plastic drainpipe · Gravel

INTERLOCKING BLOCK

A brickyard or home center will have a variety of interlocking blocks designed for retaining walls. Each style of block has its own connecting system. Some have plastic anchoring pins that are driven into the ground through holes in the block. Others simply rest on top of each other, with tabs that hook onto the courses below.

If the wall will be more than 2 feet high, batter it back for extra strength (*see pages 62–63*). Some interlocking block systems fit together so that the block on top sits an inch or so behind the block below.

LAY OUT AND INSTALL A GRAVEL BED:
Use stakes and mason's line to mark the area to be excavated, and dig away all the turf. Excavate a trench about 8 inches deep and a foot wider than the block. Lay landscaping fabric against the back of the trench and fill the trench with gravel to within a few inches of the top. Tamp it firmly with a hand tamper or the end of a 4×4. Install a perforated drainpipe that slopes away from the site toward a receptacle or an area that can disperse the runoff.

STACK THE BLOCKS: Set the first row of blocks on the gravel, twisting and tapping them as necessary to get them level and stable. You may have to add or scrape away some gravel to keep a block from wobbling. Follow the manufacturer's directions for locking the blocks together. Stack the next courses as well. When you reach the top, you can use special capping blocks for a finished appearance.

BACKFILL: Every few courses, backfill the wall with gravel. Finish the top two courses with soil if you're planning to plant. Tamp the soil lightly—flowers won't thrive in packed soil.

LANDSCAPE TIMBERS

Because landscape timbers often are exposed to moisture, they must be extremely resistant to rot. Use railroad ties or pressure-treated lumber designated for ground contact. Cut large timbers with a chain saw or cut all four sides with a circular saw, then cut the inside with a reciprocating saw or handsaw. You can stain pressure-treated wood to look like redwood (*see page 19*) after it's installed.

LAY OUT AND EXCAVATE: Dig a trench about as deep as the lumber is thick. Shovel 4 to 6 inches of gravel into the main trench, check to see that it is level, and tamp it with a hand tamper or a piece of 4×4.

LAY THE FIRST COURSE: Prepare the timbers for the bottom course by boring ½-inch holes every 2 feet. Set the timbers in the main trench, and make sure they are level along the length and across the width. In this and all other courses, leave a ¼-inch gap at the joints so water can easily seep through the wall. Drive lengths of ½-inch concrete reinforcing bar (rebar)—about 2 feet long—through the holes and into the soil. Use a 2-pound sledgehammer to drive the rebar.

SECOND COURSE: Cut and position the second course of timbers so the joints are staggered at least a foot from the joints of the first course. Set them so their front edge is ½ inch behind the front face of the first course. Drill ¼-inch holes about every 2 feet. Drive barn spikes that are about twice as long as the thickness of the timbers down through the second course and into the bottom course.

OTHER COURSES: Lay the next courses in the same way. Stagger the joints, check often for level, set each course ½ inch back from the course beneath it, and drive spikes to tie the wall together.

DEADMEN: If you're building a retaining wall more than 2 feet high, strengthen it with "deadmen"—perpendicular timbers attached to parallel timbers set in trenches in the slope. Dig the trenches at the third or fourth course and about 6 feet back into the slope—at a depth that will make them even with the course they attach to. Cut and lay 6-foot-long timbers in the trenches. Fasten the deadmen to the wall and rear timbers with 12-inch spikes or rebar driven through them.

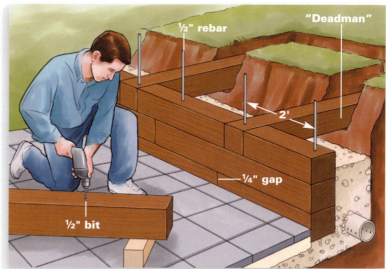

The first course of timbers will be at least partially below grade. Be sure it rests on a thick bed of gravel so water can drain away. Install perforated drainpipe to carry the water away.

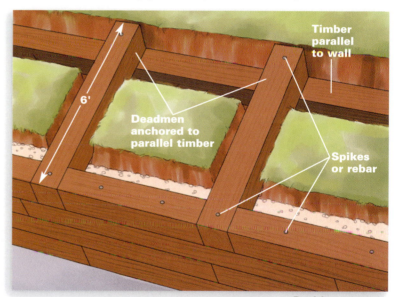

Position perpendicular deadmen every 4 feet or so to anchor the wall. Without deadmen, frost heave and water pressure can cause the wall to bulge outward. Anchor the deadmen to the hill by pinning them to timber set parallel to the wall.

RETAINING WALL OPTIONS

Some interlocking concrete blocks are shaped to form attractive curves. If you use them for retaining walls shorter than 3 feet, no drainage is necessary: Water will simply seep through the face of the wall. You won't need to use rebar with these blocks.

A brick planter adds another level to a flat yard. Walls less than 3 feet high need be only one brick thick, unless, like this one, they are capped with a flat-laid top course for seating. Brick walls taller than 3 feet must be two bricks thick. The gravel surface surrounding the planter allows access for easier weeding and flower care.

This octagonal deck extension reaches out to the surrounding view. Perimeter seating provides a forum for large-group conversation. The extension is two steps below the main deck level, establishing it as a separate space.

Furniture & Planters

A long, curving planter also is a permanent bench. It blends in visually with the curve of the deck. A large space like this needs a bit of color to break up the muted tones of wood and brick, so the owners decided to purchase bright furniture instead of building pieces to match.

Every deck or patio—no matter how beautiful it is—is incomplete without furnishings. Those furnishings should complement the landscape design as well as your lifestyle, meeting your standards of aesthetics and practicality.

Consider how you use your deck or patio. Maybe you would use it more if it had a permanent eating or food preparation area. For daily use, you need furnishings that belong to the deck or patio, whether portable or fixed.

Be flexible when planning your patio furniture. Allow for seating in areas of sunshine and shade, suitable for large or small gatherings. This flexibility will help extend the use of your deck or patio.

Planters help harmonize decks and patios with the surrounding landscape, adding the gentle touch of plants. Position planters so flowers will brighten your space without interfering with the view of the yard.

ATTACHED BENCHES

Because its supports are partly hidden by the overhanging slats, this backless bench appears to float above the deck.

Versatility is the key to these bench designs—even though they're permanent. You can adapt the backless bench, *below*, to a patio by anchoring it to 4×4 posts sunk in the ground. The backed-bench design, *opposite*, uses existing deck posts for support and provides a useful substitute for a railing section.

There are some general rules for building benches. First, the seat height should be comfortable—15 to 17 inches from the surface. Second, consider the view from the bench location. It should be where it encourages conversation. Third, make the benches safe. The back of an attached bench—used instead of a railing—usually needs to be at least 42 inches high and cannot have open spaces wider than 4 inches (check with your local building department for bench-design requirements).

A BACKLESS BENCH

Use a backless bench on a patio, a low-lying platform deck or as a transition on a multilevel deck. Check local codes for height restrictions. The bench, *left*, with its support partially hidden by the overhanging slats, appears to float above the deck surface. Its 24-inch depth offers plenty of space for sitting and for resting food and drinks.

We've mounted it to the edge of a deck. You can bolt the posts to interior joists after removing the decking, notching it, and replacing it. This design uses decking screws as fasteners; carriage bolts and lag screws will provide stronger joints. They require additional drilling, however, and may not work if your deck construction won't allow you to get a wrench on them.

CUT POSTS AND FRAMING PIECES: Construct enough supports to install one every 4 to 5 feet. For each, cut a 4×6 post, a 2×6 front support, and seat cleats. Make sure the front support is long enough to reach from the bottom of the deck joist to a height of 15 to 17 inches. Miter the ends of the seat cleats at 22½ degrees. (For a patio bench, cut the posts at 15 to 17 inches and bolt 2×6 feet to both sides.)

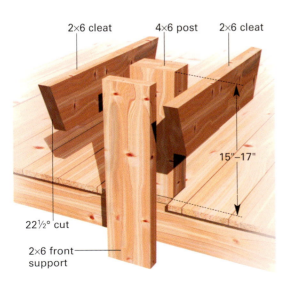

2×6 cleat   4×6 post   2×6 cleat

15"–17"

22½° cut

2×6 front support

Assemble each support from a 4×6 post and three 2×6s. Notch the decking so the front support can be attached to the deck joist or fascia.

Clamp 2×2s as an overhang guide; use ½-inch plywood for spacers. Adjust the spacing before attaching the last slats.

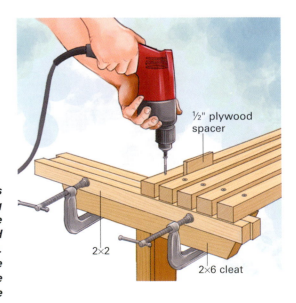

½" plywood spacer

2×2

2×6 cleat

ASSEMBLE THE SUPPORTS: Fasten the two post sections—flush at the tops—with six or seven 3-inch deck screws driven into predrilled pilot holes. Then center one cleat on the laminated post, hold it flush at the top, and fasten it with four or five 3-inch deck screws through predrilled pilot holes. Attach the other 2×6 cleat in the same way.

FASTEN THE SUPPORTS: The front support needs to be snug against the deck joist, so notch the decking if necessary. Use a post level to plumb the post in both directions (see page 16). Predrill pilot holes at an angle through the 4×6 and through the face of the 2×6 beam, then drive 3-inch decking screws through the post and front support.

INSTALL THE SEAT SLATS: Cut twelve 2×2s to a length that will overhang each cleat by 3 inches. In order to keep the overhang consistent, clamp two 2×2s to the side of the cleat. Lay the slats on a flat surface and mark pilot holes so they will be centered on the cleats. Start the first slat with a ¼-inch overhang on the front of the cleats and fasten it with 3-inch deck screws at each support. Fasten the remaining seat slats, using scraps of ½-inch plywood as spacers.

SEAT WITH BACK

This design uses existing rail posts for part of the framing. You can attach the bench without altering balusters or rails with most rail designs. However, the seat may look better if you remove all the balusters (building codes permitting, of course). If the rail posts are spaced more than 6 feet apart, install intervening posts (see page 30).

INSTALL THE SEAT SUPPORTS: Each support requires two 25-inch 2×4 cleats—mitered on one end at 22½ degrees—and one 15-inch 4×4 seat post. Cut the pieces and mark both sides of the rail post 15 inches above the decking. Have a helper hold a 2×4 level at the mark while you drill pilot holes and drive three 3-inch deck screws. Attach the other 2×4 to the other side of the post. Then fasten the 4×4 post with two screws on each side and with angled screws to the deck.

CUT AND INSTALL THE BACK BRACE: Use a circular saw to cut a 4×4 to the dimensions shown. Attach the back support to the rail post with several screws.

INSTALL THE SEAT AND BACK SLATS: Cut three 2×4s for the back and three 2×6s for the seat to the length of the bench (overhanging them 3 inches, if possible). Space them evenly and attach them to the 2×4s with two 3-inch screws driven into each joint.

Anchor this seat to the rail posts for support. Use 2×4s for the back and 2×6s for seat slats. Place the bench where it can be part of a conversation area or where it faces a pleasant view.

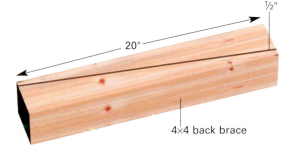

20"
½"
4×4 back brace

Use a chalk line or straightedge to mark the angled rip cut for the back brace. Mark both sides and make the cut with a circular saw. This cut is difficult; practice on a scrap first.

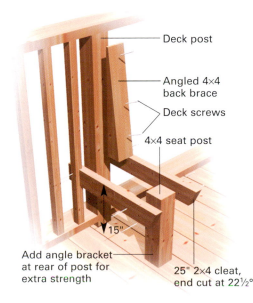

Deck post
Angled 4×4 back brace
Deck screws
4×4 seat post
15"
Add angle bracket at rear of post for extra strength
25" 2×4 cleat, end cut at 22½°

Mark the deck post 15 inches from the decking, and attach the cleats at the mark. Level and attach the seat post between the 2×4s and to the decking. Install the back brace with its bottom edge flush with the top of the cleats. Then fasten the back and seat slats.

FREESTANDING BENCHES

This bench, with its wide slats, will provide plenty of sturdy comfort and can easily be moved around the deck or patio surface.

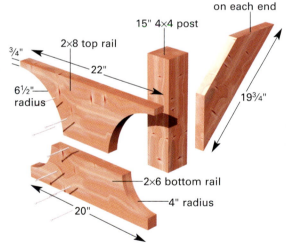

Benches made of standard lumber will not be lightweight, but they will be stable. And you'll be surprised how easily you can move them about your deck or patio to respond to changing shade patterns or entertainment needs.

"PICNIC-STYLE" BENCH

With its wide slats and-shaped legs, this bench is reminiscent of a picnic table, and its design allows a bit of versatility, too. Make the bench permanent by attaching it to joists below the decking, or by setting posts in footings next to a platform deck or patio.

In a permanent installation, you can dispense with the bottom rails and braces, unless you want to keep the braces for a decorative touch. Choose any length, and install a support every 4 feet.

CUT THE SCALLOPED RAILS: Each support requires a 22-inch 2×8 top rail and a 20-inch 2×6 bottom rail. (For more strength, install two rails on each side of the posts.) Cut the pieces to the proper length. Then mark and cut each end of one top and one bottom rail. For the top rail, set a compass at 6½ inches and—with the compass point just at the corner of the board—mark the scallop outline on both ends as shown.

Cut the 4×4 post and the top and bottom rails, and attach them with deck screws. Fasten the brace after you attach the seat slats.

2×6 brace, cut at 45° on each end

15" 4×4 post

¾"

2×8 top rail

22"

6½" radius

19¾"

2×6 bottom rail

4" radius

20"

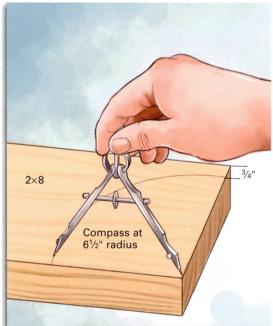

2×8

¾"

Compass at 6½" radius

To scallop the top and bottom rails, set a compass just at the corner of the board and draw the arc.

BUYING FACTORY-MADE WOODEN OUTDOOR FURNITURE

You may find wooden benches and picnic tables at a local deck yard priced only slightly higher than the cost of materials to build your own. Carefully check out the quality of the lumber and the fasteners; they may be wanting. You may be able to make a flimsy piece solid by strategically drilling pilot holes and driving a few screws. Don't buy pieces that have warped or cracked wood. You may be able to beautify and make untreated lumber rot-resistant by applying a stain or sealer (*see page 19*).

Use the same technique to mark the bottom rail, setting the compass at 4 inches. Make all the cuts with a saber saw, then sand the curved cuts smooth. Use the first pieces as templates for marking the others.

CUT THE POSTS AND BRACES: For each support, cut a 15-inch 4×4 post and a 19¾-inch 2×6 brace. Miter each end of the brace at 45 degrees.

ASSEMBLE THE SUPPORTS: Assemble the 2×8 top rails so they form a T flush with the top of the post and overhang by 9¼ inches on each side. Drill pilot holes and drive four 3-inch deck screws. Attach the bottom rail in the same fashion, flush with the bottom edge of the post and overhanging it by 8¼ inches.

CUT AND ATTACH THE SEAT SLATS: Cut the three 2×8 slats to length. Then set your compass at 7¼ inches. Center the point of the compass on the width of one slat with the pencil just touching the end of the slat. Mark the curve on the corners, cut the curves with a saber saw, and sand smooth.

Lay the seat slats on the support assemblies. (Have a helper keep things from toppling over.) Attach them at ¼-inch intervals with three 3-inch deck screws.

ATTACH THE BRACES: Turn the bench upside down and have a helper check each support for square as you position the angle-cut braces. Drill pilot holes and drive deck screws through the braces into the posts. Make sure each brace is centered on the middle seat slat, then fasten the braces with screws driven through the slat.

Then, cut the legs (one 15-inch and one 11½-inch 2×4 for each leg) and predrill them every 6 inches in a zigzag pattern so the screws won't split the wood along a grain line. Spread a thin layer of glue and drive the screws. Then laminate two legs, notch side down, to a 48-inch slat with a 41-inch slat between the legs. Laminate the rest of the 48-inch slats until you have only one left. Then fasten the remaining pair of legs, notch up, with a 41-inch slat between them. Finish the bench with the final 48-inch slat. When the glue has dried completely, sand the surfaces smooth.

Use a belt sander to get the surface smooth and level. (Be careful—a belt sander can remove a lot of wood quickly.)

Take the time to sand the top of the bench smooth. Apply several coats of sealer, with no spaces between the slats—water may puddle.

BUTCHER-BLOCK BENCH

This design adapts butcher-block-table construction to create a multipurpose addition to your deck or patio. Increase the impact by building a companion coffee table using use the same design and shortening the legs.

CHOOSE A LAMINATING METHOD: The seat slats and the legs are made by laminating 2×4s side by side with glue and predrilled 2¾-inch screws. Before you start, stack the slats in position and mark the sides of each pair for the screws. Stagger the marks so you won't drive screws on top of each other.

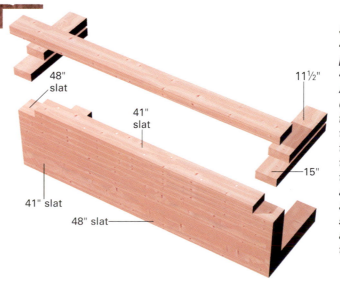

48" slat

41" slat

41" slat

48" slat

11½"

15"

Start with a 48-inch slat, leg pieces, and a 41-inch slat. Align each slat carefully—flush at the top—and mark the positions; then laminate them with glue and screws. Stagger the screws to avoid splitting the wood.

OUTDOOR TABLES

This outdoor table design can be adjusted for multiple duties. Lengthen the legs and build it as a food preparation counter. Shorten the legs to construct a coffee table.

W hen the temperature is right and the sky is clear, eating outdoors is a rustic joy—all the more so if your outdoor dining area is as convenient as the one you use indoors.

Here's a table that fits the bill— large enough for small groups and hardy enough to stand up to the rough treatment of the elements and outdoor use.

Construct the tabletop with lumber that is smooth and nearly free of knots; choose boards with a close grain so that the top will be easy to wipe and won't splinter. Use a

naturally rot-resistant species of wood or stain pressure-treated lumber to improve its looks.

DINING TABLE

If the benches or chairs you'll use have seats 16 to 17 inches high, make your table 29 to 30 inches high—the standard for indoor dining. If your benches are lower, adjust the table height accordingly. (If in doubt, make it higher—you can always trim the legs later.) Four to six diners can use a table that is 44 inches wide and 62 inches long.

Make each support from 4×4s and 2×4s fastened with lag screws and washers. The more precisely you cut the framing pieces, the tighter and stronger the joints will be.

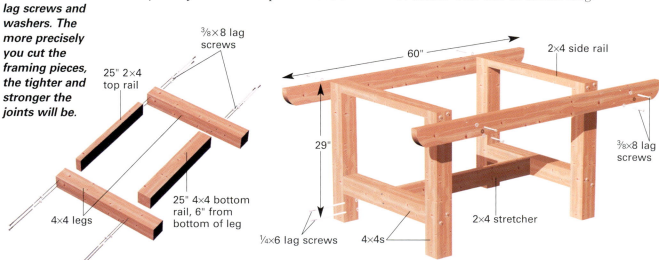

Overhang the side rails on the leg assemblies by at least 10 inches so a person sitting at the end will have enough leg room.

CUT THE LEG ASSEMBLIES: All the framing pieces must butt together tightly to make strong joints, so cut them precisely. Have the lumberyard or home center make the cuts if they can guarantee accuracy. If you will be cutting with a circular saw, practice cutting scrap 4×4s until you can produce cuts that are square all around; you may have to adjust the base-plate so the blade is exactly square to the base plate.

For each of the two leg assemblies, cut a 2×4 top rail and a 4×4 bottom rail, each to 25 inches. Cut two 4×4 legs to the height of the table, less 1½ inches.

ASSEMBLE THE LEGS: Lay the pieces on a flat surface and clamp the four assemblies together with a long bar clamp or pipe clamp. Check for square before you start drilling.

Position the top rail flush with the tops of the legs, and the bottom rail 6 inches from the bottom of the legs. Drill pilot holes and attach the legs to the rails with ⅜×8-inch lag screws and washers.

BUILD THE TABLE FRAME: Cut a 2×4 stretcher 27 inches shorter than the overall length of the table—35 inches for a table that will be 62 inches long. Stand the two leg assemblies up, and attach the stretcher between them with two ¼×6-inch lag screws at each end.

Next, miter at 45 degrees two 2×4 side rails 2 inches shorter than the length of the table, and attach them to the posts with two lag screws at each joint. The side rails should run past the legs by 10 inches on each side. Now you're ready for the tabletop.

ATTACH THE TOP: Cut all the 2×6 top pieces to length (44 inches in this design), and attach them centered on the side rails with 3-inch deck screws or 16d galvanized nails. Sand the edges smooth.

OUTDOOR WORKTABLE

An outdoor worktable like the one shown on this page can be a great time saver for potting and other gardening chores—even for preparing outdoor meals. The shelf below is large enough for buckets or bags. Rounded corners on the front of the backsplash add a small, effective decorative detail.

A worktable countertop should be 35 to 37 inches high. Even if you will be using it for rough gardening work, use wood that is smooth and free of large knots so you can wipe it easily.

CONSTRUCT THE FRAME: Cut 2×4 legs to the height of the table minus ¾ inch, and cut 2×4 crossbraces for the top and bottom.

Assemble the frame on a flat surface with two 3-inch deck screws into each joint. Use a framing square as you work.

ADD THE TOP, SHELF, AND BACK: For both the table and the shelf, cut 1×6s or 1×8s to fit; attach them with 8d galvanized nails or 2-inch deck screws. Use a saber saw to cut the rounded front edges of the 1×10 backsplash, and attach it to the top rails with the same-sized nails or screws.

A practical table with a shelf beneath can serve a multitude of purposes. If you like, add another shelf in the middle.

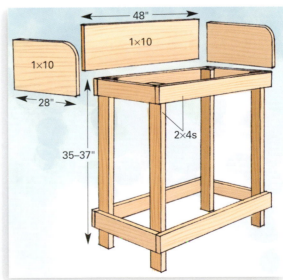

48"

1×10

1×10

28"

2×4s

35–37"

The framing is simple. Take the time to check each joint for square before fastening.

GARDEN BENCH

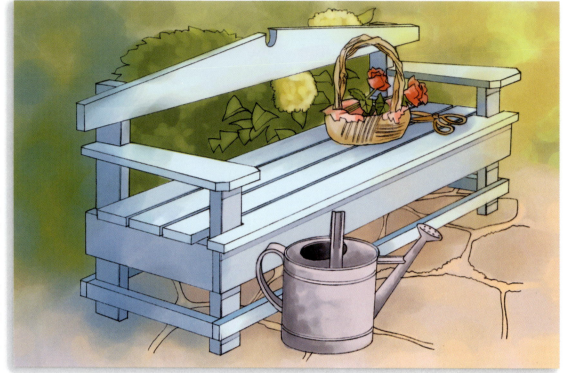

This bench will be strong and easily moved around for the best possible view. Five-quarter lumber will reduce the weight and lighten its appearance as well.

This bench has the look of crafted furniture but, in fact, its construction does not require fancy joinery. It does, however, require precise cuts. Rent or buy a power miter box (also called a chop saw), which makes perfectly square cuts with ease.

Use top-grade wood that won't warp, shrink, or splinter. Kiln-dried clear or B-grade redwood is an excellent choice; cedar heartwood is another. Choose boards with close, straight grain.

The design calls for some ⁵⁄₄ (five-quarter) lumber, which is actually 1 inch thick. Standard 1× stock would be too thin; you can use 2× lumber, but the bench will be heavy and less graceful. You may be able to find ⁵⁄₄×6 decking; you'll probably need to have the ⁵⁄₄×8 stock for the backrest specially milled. If milling costs are a problem, make the backrest from a 2×8.

CUT THE BACK AND ARMRESTS

Use a circular saw or table saw to cut the three pieces to the dimensions shown, tapering the outer edge of the armrest from 5½ inches to 2¾ inches. Cut the 2-inch rounded notch at the top of the seat back with a saber saw. Use a sanding block to round all of the edges slightly so they won't be sharp.

If you use different designs for the armrest and backrest, make them complementary. For example, if you round the front corners of the armrests, also round the end corners of the backrest.

Make an angled rip cut along the outside edge of the armrest. Clamp the boards securely before making long cuts such as these; practice on scrap pieces if you're not sure you can cut straight lines.

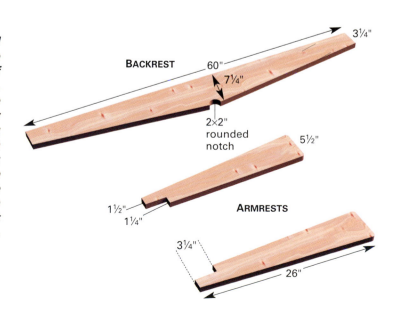

BACKREST   60"   3¼"

7¼"

2×2" rounded notch

5½"

1½"
1¼"

ARMRESTS

3¼"

26"

BUILD THE FRAME

Use ⁵⁄₄ lumber for the horizontal framing members and 2×4s for the posts. Cut the rear posts to 32 inches and the front posts to 23 inches. Cut notches ³⁄₈ inch deep and 1 inch high in the two rear posts for the notched end of the arm rests, *below*. The arm rests need to fit snugly, so make precise cuts. (For information on cutting notches, see page 30.)

With a helper, assemble the frame on a flat surface. Check each joint for square before drilling pilot holes and driving 2½-inch deck screws. First attach the side rails to the posts with the edges flush at front and rear; then attach the front and back rails. Notice that the top back rail is cut shorter than the front rail and is fastened inside the rear posts. Finally, measure the distance between the front and rear rails and cut and install the center block between the rails.

ADD THE SEAT SLATS, ARMRESTS, AND BACKREST

Cut the seat slats so they overhang the frame by an inch on both sides. Notch both ends of the front slat so it fits around the front posts. Lay the slats on the frame evenly spaced, and attach them by drilling pilot holes and driving 2½-inch deck screws.

Have a helper hold the backrest so it overhangs the posts by the same amount on each side. Make sure the bottom is level. Drill pilot holes and drive two 2½-inch deck screws through the backrest into the posts.

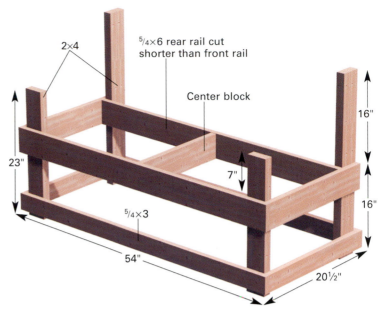

Before you attach the armrest, fit each one into the grooves in the rear post—positioned exactly as they will be when fastened. Drill two pilot holes in the front of the armrest into the posts and one pilot hole in the thin side of the rear notch, *below*.

To attach each armrest, spread polyurethane glue into the grooves in the rear posts and on the top of the front posts. Slip the notched end of the armrest into the groove. Drive 2½-inch deck screws through the pilot holes.

Sand all sharp edges to prevent splintering. Apply a stain and sealer, or two or three coats of exterior enamel paint.

This design calls for ⁵⁄₄ (five-quarter) lumber for horizontal framing members. If you use 2×6s and 2×3s instead, increase the length of the fasteners.

Position the seat slats so they overhang 1 inch on each side and in front, and so the gaps between them are equal. Before attaching the backrest, make sure it is centered and that the bottom edge is level.

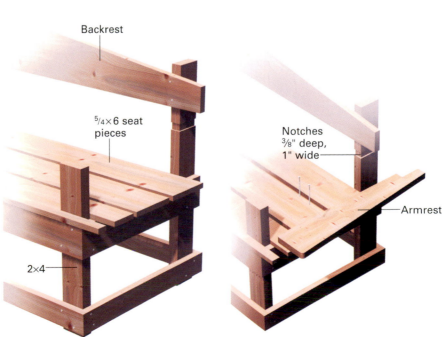

Attach the armrests with polyurethane glue and carefully placed screws. The notches must be cut precisely to support the armrests.

PLANTERS

This bench and planter combination is large enough to hold small trees as well as flowers. The gaps between the bench slats permit water to run through, reducing the possibility of rot.

Planters put deck and patio gardening within easy reach. Make them small enough so you can easily reach all of the soil and high enough so you don't strain your knees and back.

These planter projects are designed to hold soil, but you can use them for holding flower-pots as well—shuffle the foliage around and put your showiest flowers in prominent places. Use the same designs shown here, and size them so your pots can fit snugly inside.

You can build several planters in a day with a circular saw, drill, and basic carpentry skills. Just make sure that you start with all the materials on hand.

PLANTER-BENCH

A combination planter and bench lets you tend your plants while comfortably seated or is simply a pleasant spot to enjoy the foliage.

If you want a longer unit, build three or more boxes of the same size, and position them either in a row or form a right-angle corner. Install seat slats between them.

START THE BOXES: For each box, cut nineteen 2×4s to the same length—24 inches is recommended. Working on a flat surface,

make square frames with lapped ends, *opposite*. Fasten the lapped ends with two 3-inch deck screws at each joint.

Next make a bottom with 1×4s. Cut the pieces to fit, and fasten them to one of the 2×4 frames with ⅛-inch gaps for drainage.

Stack two courses of 2×4 frames on the one to which the bottom is attached, and fasten a 16-inch length of 2×2 to all the frame corners by driving 2½-inch screws into predrilled holes. Build the other box(es) to the third course using the same techniques.

BUILD THE BENCH: This design requires spacers to separate the bench slats. Cut eighteen ¼- to ½-inch-by-3½-inch-square spacers from exterior plywood. Then cut seven 2×4 bench slats to the length you want the bench. Set the first slat on the third course of each box, and attach it to the 2×2 corner brace. Fasten the remaining slats to each other by driving 3-inch screws through the spacers inserted between the slats.

FINISH THE PLANTERS: When the bench is completed, cut 2×4 fillers to fit between the last bench slat and the box corner. Screw them to the corner brace and to the bench slat. Then complete each box by attaching the last 2×4 frames to the corner braces.

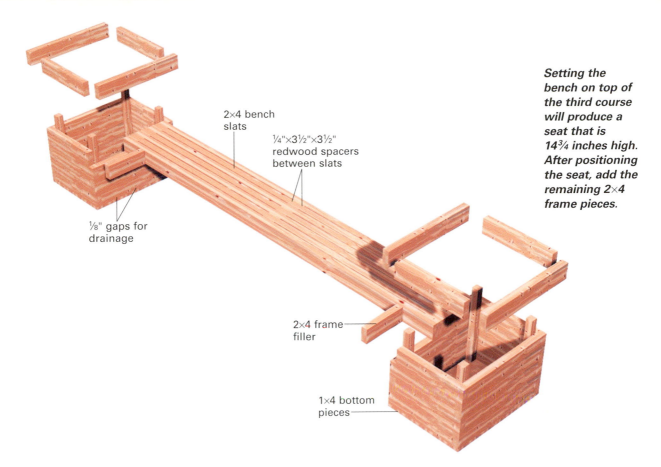

2×4 bench slats

¼"×3½"×3½" redwood spacers between slats

Setting the bench on top of the third course will produce a seat that is 14¾ inches high. After positioning the seat, add the remaining 2×4 frame pieces.

⅛" gaps for drainage

2×4 frame filler

1×4 bottom pieces

2×2 corner braces tie all the planter pieces together. Drive a screw through the braces into each 2×4.

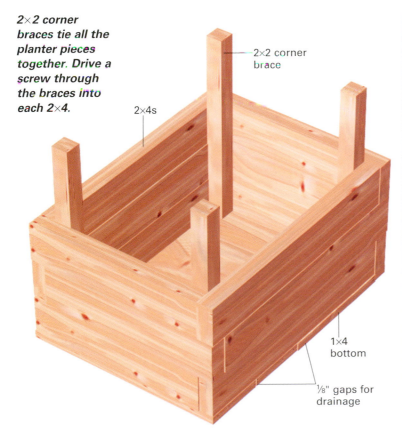

2×2 corner brace

2×4s

1×4 bottom

⅛" gaps for drainage

A large planting area made of dry-laid boulders can have space for trees and shrubs as well as smaller plants. Gravel surrounding the plants harmonizes with the boulders and cuts down on the need to weed. Boulders this large must be installed with earth-moving machinery.

PLANTERS
continued

Fill this planter with soil or place potted plants in it. The legs allow air to circulate under the planter so there is less chance of damage to the deck or patio surface.

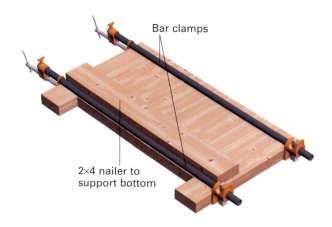

Bar clamps

2×4 nailer to support bottom

Practice clamping and gluing so that you know just how much glue to apply. There should be a small amount of squeezed-out glue; allow it to dry, then chip it away. Your can add 2×4 nailers (before the glue sets) on the interior for increased strength.

PLANTER WITH LEGS

This planter partially relies on glue to hold the pieces together. Use polyurethane glue, which has remarkable holding power; it will keep boards fused together even in climates with severe winters.

These dimensions produce a planter that will stand 3 inches off the deck or patio surface. Change the length of the corner pieces if you want shorter or longer legs.

MAKE THE SIDES: Cut five 14-inch 2×4s for each side and two 17-inch 2×4s for each leg. Working on a flat surface covered with a drop cloth, spread glue along the edges of the boards. Clamp the sides with two pipe clamps or bar clamps. Make sure the tops and bottoms are flush, and allow them to dry. Scrape away squeezed-out glue when it is partially dry. Do the same for the other sides.

ASSEMBLE THE PIECES: Stand the sides up and nail or screw them together at the corners. At the bottom inside edge of each side, attach 2×4 nailers by drilling pilot holes and driving two 2½-inch deck screws into each joint. Cut a piece of ¾-inch pressure-treated plywood to fit in the bottom. Drill a grid of ⅜-inch holes for drainage, and set it in the bottom. Attach the bottom with screws driven from the outside of the box.

You don't have to hide your pots in planters. Clay pots have a charming appearance and they let you move your foliage at will. Wall-hung containers embellish an otherwise plain surface with splashes of color.

PLANTER WITH GROOVE DESIGN

A simple geometric design takes less than an hour to build and adds style to a plain planter. It's made by cutting grooves in the finished surface, or you can attach molding or 1×2s symmetrically to the outside of the planter.

MAKE THE PLANTER: Miter-cut four pieces of 2×12 to the same length—18 inches is recommended. Attach the corners by drilling pilot holes and driving 12d casing nails. Cut 1×4s for the bottom—½ inch shorter than the width of the box—and attach them with nails or screws so they are recessed ¼ inch all around. (Lay the 1×4s out on the box before you attach them—you may have to rip the end pieces for the recess.)

CUT THE GROOVES: Use a framing square to draw cut lines for parallel and perpendicular grooves. In our example, the grooves are ⅜ inch wide and are spaced 3 inches from the edges of the planter in both directions.

Set your circular saw to the desired depth (in this case, ⅜ inch), and use a speed square as a guide to make straight cuts along the lines. It will take three or more passes with the saw blade to produce a groove that is ⅜ inch wide.

Although it may appear complicated, this planter can be quickly built with common carpentry tools. If you are unsure of your ability to make precise 45-degree corner miters, practice on scrap.

Placed in front of ground-level windows filled with glass block, this mortared tile planter enlivens a drab spot with a splash of color. The tiles cover a cement-block wall. Flowers planted in the block recesses add pleasant contrasts.

Draw lines to mark the sides of each groove. Carefully set the blade of a circular saw to the correct depth. Cut the grooves. Each groove requires several passes.

This complicated looking pool and fountain require only a few basic skills to install. Start with a pool liner like the one on page 92, and place the pump and fountain outside of the pond. Surround the liner with mortared flagstones. Set the flagstone steps at a slight angle toward the pool to direct the water downward.

Soft low-voltage lights scattered among plants provide just enough light on this patio for late-night conversations. The standard-voltage lights attached to the house provide additional illumination.

OUTDOOR AMENITIES

An outdoor room—that's what your patio or deck really is—can combine the beauty and spaciousness of the outdoors with many comforts of an indoor living space. Some indoor amenities are worth adding, such as electrical receptacles. If you love outdoor cooking, running water and a sink enhance the utility and enjoyment of your space.

Outdoor lighting adds decorative beauty as well as extra hours to the enjoyment of a deck or patio. Easily installed low-voltage systems can provide just the right mood.

Outdoor kitchens get the heat of cooking out of the kitchen and allow the cook to enjoy more time with the guests. An outdoor cooking area with a propane grill and some cabinetry will be nearly as easy to use as the one indoors. With a working sink outdoors, you can cook entire meals without dashing in and out of the house. This chapter shows you how to connect to household utility systems to complete the basic installation.

Just off the deck or patio, a small pool with a fountain adds charm. Research the project, however, to find plants and fish suitable to your climate—species that require a minimum of maintenance.

And speaking of species, nothing adds color and interest to an outdoor setting like birds. This chapter shows you how to keep them sheltered and fed.

A fully equipped outdoor kitchen lets the cook mingle with guests while preparing the meal. A high counter serves as a buffet or eating area and helps to keep small children safely away from a hot grill.

ADDING ELECTRICAL SERVICE

Install a ground fault circuit interrupter (GFCI) receptacle in all outdoor receptacles. GFCIs sense small changes in the current (caused by shorts or human contact) and immediately disconnect power to the circuit. All outdoor boxes should be weathertight.

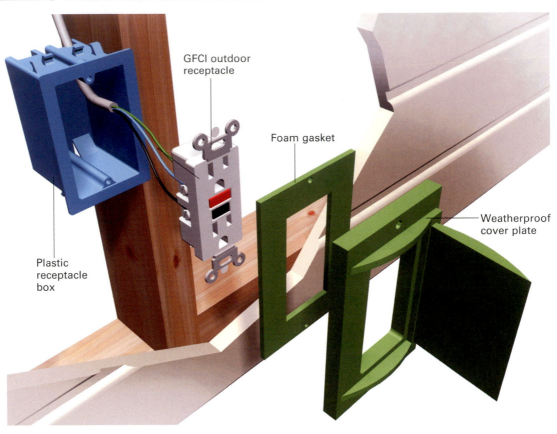

GFCI outdoor receptacle

Foam gasket

Weatherproof cover plate

Plastic receptacle box

Weathertight boxes are sealed with weatherproof gaskets and conduit fittings to ensure that water will not short out the circuit.

Weatherproof outlet box

Adding an outdoor receptacle to your deck or patio area can add a number of indoor conveniences to your outdoor room. Low-voltage lighting will extend the usefulness of your deck into the evening hours.

Low-voltage lighting systems are virtually foolproof and require only some minor skills to install. Adding an outlet to a household circuit is a bit more complicated. (If you're inexperienced at adding an outlet, it's better to research other resource manuals before starting your project.)

Remember the cardinal rule for all electrical jobs: Before beginning your work, shut off the power to the circuit at the service panel and test the circuit to make sure the power is really off.

If you're extending a circuit, check your local building codes for materials and installation requirements.

WIRE AN OUTDOOR RECEPTACLE

The easiest way to install an outdoor receptacle is to place it on the outside wall roughly (but not directly) opposite a receptacle on the inside. Make sure the new receptacle will not overload the circuit. (Add up the amperage of the existing and new appliances; the total should not exceed the rating of the breaker for that circuit.)

DRILL A HOLE: Shut off the power, remove the interior receptacle cover plate, and test to make sure the power is off. Pull the receptacle out of the way. Punch out a knockout hole (a prepunched-but-covered hole for cable entry) in the rear of the junction box and angle a long drill bit through it. Bore a hole from inside through the exterior wall—this will mark the location of the junction box for your new outdoor receptacle. Use a masonry bit when boring through brick or concrete.

CUT THE HOLE: Cut a hole in the siding for the new box. Use a saber saw if the siding is wood. In masonry, drill around the perimeter of the box, then punch out the middle with a hammer and a cold chisel.

RUN THE CABLE: This can be difficult. Have a helper on one side. Push through the cable, then strip, wire, and clamp it to both boxes.

Low-voltage system transformer

GFCI outdoor receptacle

Low-voltage lighting is inexpensive and easy to install. Different systems will cast light on almost any outdoor area or feature. After you've laid out and installed the fixtures, run the cable in a shallow trench.

INSTALL A WEATHERPROOF RECEPTACLE:
Attach the new box with screws, or pack mortar around it in a masonry wall. Install a ground fault circuit interrupter (GFCI) receptacle with a weatherproof cover. Turn the power back on at the service panel.

LOW-VOLTAGE LIGHTING

The easiest way to add exterior lights is to buy a low-voltage lighting kit, which includes cable, lights, and a transformer that steps the voltage down so it is safe to the touch.

Some kits are designed to light patio surfaces, walkways, and stairways. Others show off plantings, walls, or fountains. Purchase a kit with a timer or a photovoltaic switch to turn the lights on automatically when it gets dark.

Mount the transformer near an outdoor receptacle where it won't be damaged, on the wall or on the same post as the receptacle, if possible.

Lay out the light fixtures and poke the mounting stakes into the ground. Dig a shallow trench for the cable, lay it in, and cover it. Plug the transformer into the receptacle.

If you want to place lights on a railing or a fence, run the cable where it is out of the way, and fasten it with cable staples about every foot, so it won't dangle. Use mounting plates that are designed for installing light fixtures on a horizontal surface.

Mounting plate

To install low-voltage lights on a railing, purchase a kit with mounting plates. Drill the hole, then install the plate with the screws provided.

Cable staples

Run low-voltage cable alongside posts and under rails, or wherever it will be least visible. Fasten it with round-topped cable staples; standard square-topped staples may cut the cable.

BARBECUE CABINET AND COUNTERTOP

Place a barbecue cabinet where you can easily tap into your home's electrical and plumbing lines. Consider the location of the grill first. Most propane grills must be at least 1 foot from combustible surfaces.

This versatile outdoor kitchen setup will make outdoor cooking easier, so you'll probably do more of it. A counter next to the grill makes preparation easier and gets the cook out of the kitchen and into the open air. Guests and family members will have more fun helping with the food preparation.

PROVIDE PLUMBING AND ELECTRICAL SERVICE

With its sink and refrigerator, this cabinet brings kitchen convenience outdoors so you won't have to make as many trips inside. You can wash vegetables in the 15-inch-square bar sink, and then wash your hands. The wiring and electrical work can be complicated, so plan carefully or hire a professional.

If you install the cabinet on a deck or patio extension, you can run the utility lines underground—good design and planning will save time and money later.

PLUMBING: Connect copper water lines for the sink by tapping into interior pipes that run on an outside wall of the house.

Install a separate shut-off valve for each line so you can easily turn the water off from inside. Where winters are severe, have a way to drain the outside lines so the pipes won't freeze and burst.

Connecting the drain line into the house drainage system can be complicated. Check with local codes and be sure the drain line is properly vented (this usually requires the sink to be within 5 feet of a vented stack and installing a vent loop).

If you will use the sink only occasionally, you may want to have the drainpipe empty into the yard. If so, use only biodegradable soap when you wash. Or, have the drainpipe lead to a dry well—a hole in the ground that is under the level of the sink, about 2 feet in diameter and 4 feet deep, filled with gravel and covered with landscaping fabric and sod.

ELECTRICAL: Install a GFCI receptacle inside the cabinet for the refrigerator, and another one above the cabinet so you can plug in small appliances. (See page 82 for information on adding an outdoor receptacle.)

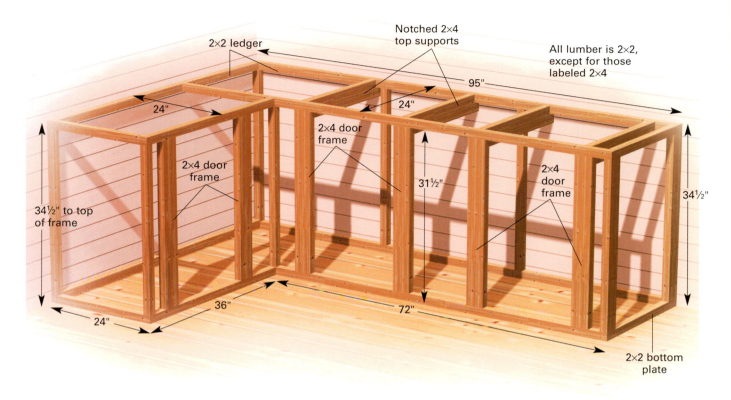

2×2 ledger

Notched 2×4 top supports

All lumber is 2×2, except for those labeled 2×4

24"

95"

24"

2×4 door frame

2×4 door frame

31½"

2×4 door frame

34½" to top of frame

34½"

36"

72"

24"

2×2 bottom plate

Make the frame with 2×2s and 2×4s. The deck or patio will serve as the cabinet floor. Use vertical 2×4s to frame each side of the door openings, then attach horizontal 2×4 headers.

FRAME THE CABINET

Before you start the cabinet framing, make sure you know the opening size for the refrigerator. You should be able to easily slip the unit into place.

Construct the cabinet framing out of 2×2s, with 2×4s for the door frames. (The 2×2s may seem spindly, but when the tongue-and-groove siding is installed, the structure will be strong.)

For a standard-size cabinet, the frame should be 34½ inches high and 24 inches deep. When measuring, always factor in the 1½-inch thickness of the frame members. For instance, the vertical 2×2s and 2×4s are cut to 31½ inches; the added thicknesses of the 2×2 top and bottom plates produces a total framing height of 34½ inches.

Sketch out a design, using this plan as a reference, and include dimensions for the framing members and openings. Choose pressure-treated stock that is straight and free of cracks. Drill pilot holes for each fastener to avoid splitting the wood.

Start by constructing the back wall framing. Cut the 2×2 ledger and framing pieces to the proper length and assemble each wall section on the deck. Attach the assembly to the house with 3-inch decking screws driven into the studs (find the studs by locating the nail lines in the siding). If the siding is brick, drill holes in the brick first, and use masonry anchors. Make sure the frame remains square as you fasten it.

Assemble the remaining frames and with a helper, position the sides, check them for square and level, and attach them to each other and to the decking with screws driven through predrilled holes. If you build on a patio, attach the 2×2 bottom plate by drilling holes and driving masonry screws.

After the entire framing is complete, cut and notch the 2×4 countertop supports so they fit under the ledger, flush with the house and flush with the top of the framing, *above*. Then cut horizontal 2×4 headers to fit between the 2×4 door frames and attach them to the door frames with screws driven at an angle (*see page 86*).

BARBEQUE CABINET AND COUNTERTOP
continued

Plan for the placement of tongue-and-groove pieces on each side of the doors so they will be even at the corners. Mark the position of the pattern across the opening.

INSTALL SIDING AND DOORS

The cabinet facing should complement the overall look of the deck, patio, and house. You can face the cabinet with the same materials as the house but you may need to compromise if things don't look compatible with the deck.

Grooved T1-11 or other sheet siding will be the easiest to install: Just cut the sheets to fit and attach them with deck screws or nails.

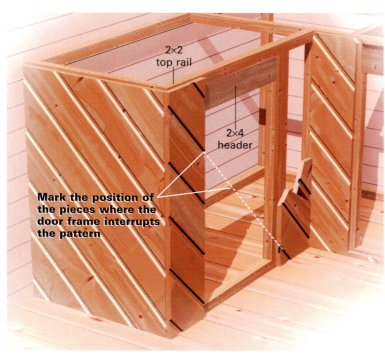

2×2 top rail

2×4 header

Mark the position of the pieces where the door frame interrupts the pattern

CABINET DOOR

Join the tongue-and-groove pieces together with polyurethane glue. Before the glue dries, attach a frame of 1×2s on the face, then 1×2s around the perimeter.

1×2 framing

1×2 edging

INSTALLING 1×4 OR 1×6 TONGUE-AND-GROOVE SIDING: Place a strip of ¼-inch plywood on the deck next to the framing to keep the bottom of the siding slightly raised above the deck or patio.

You can make the 45-degree miter cuts with a circular saw (use a speed square as a guide), but it will be easier with a power miter saw or radial arm saw. As you cut each piece of siding, use it as a template to mark the next piece before installing it. Attach the boards by drilling pilot holes and driving 4d casing nails at an angle through the base of the tongue and into the framing. Install the pieces tongue-side up.

Cut a triangular corner piece first. Nail it in place as described above. Then cut and install the remaining pieces on the rest of the framing. Where a doorway interrupts a board, *left*, use a straight board to mark the positions of the pieces on the other side of the door so the pattern will be consistent across the opening.

TRIM OUT: When the paneling is installed, attach a 1×2 filler across the doorway opening, then trim the corners, the top edge, and the door frames with 1×2 stock to cover all exposed siding ends (*see page 84*). When trimming the door openings, miter the trim corners. You can butt-joint the trim corners at the top edge and elsewhere.

MAKE THE DOORS: Cut pieces for the door facing at 45-degree angles so when they are fit together they produce a rectangle that is 1¾ inches less than both dimensions of the door opening. (When you add the 1×2 door edging to the tongue-and-groove paneling, the door will be shorter by ¼ inch all around—just right for clearance.)

Assemble the pieces temporarily (but tightly), and measure the door panel. Cut and miter four 1×2s for the face frame and four more for the perimeter edging. Working on a flat surface, apply a bead of glue on each tongue and press the pieces together. Adjust the pieces for square and attach the face and perimeter frames with glue and 3d casing nails or screws keeping edges and corners flush.

INSTALL THE DOORS: Use nails as spacers at the bottom to position the doors in the opening, leaving ⅛-inch gaps all around. Install hinges and catches.

MAKING THE COUNTERTOP

Purchase all the countertop tiles you need—regular field tiles, edging tiles, and corner edging tiles. Ask your supplier for vitreous or impervious tiles that have proven themselves durable for outdoor use in your particular climate.

BUILD THE SUBSTRATE: Cut pieces of ¾-inch pressure-treated plywood so the edges overhang the framing by about an inch all around. Attach it with screws. Cut out the opening for the sink with a saber saw. Cut pieces of ½-inch cement backerboard to fit exactly on top of the plywood. Attach it to the plywood with a grid pattern of 1¼-inch deck screws spaced 4 to 6 inches apart.

DRYRUN THE TILES: Set most of the tiles in place on top of the countertop with plastic spacers between them. This dry run allows you to make adjustments if necessary; you may be able to avoid cutting some tiles by adjusting the layout. Avoid using small slivers of tiles. Use a snap cutter to cut the tiles so your pattern is complete before you begin setting the tiles.

SET THE TILES: Mix thin-set mortar, using liquid latex additive. Remove a section of dry-laid tiles about 3 feet square. Apply the thin-set to the backerboard with a notched trowel, and set the tiles in it. Push each tile into place with a very slight twist; do not slide the tiles around. Once a section is laid, use a beater board (a short piece of 2×6 wrapped with carpeting) and a hammer to tap all the tiles down for a smooth surface. Continue this process until all the tiles are installed.

GROUT AND CLEAN: Wait at least a day for the mortar to dry. Mix sanded grout with latex additive, and apply it with a laminated grout float (one that has a squeegee-like, hard rubber face). First, hold the float nearly flat as you push the grout into the joints with sweeping motions in several directions. Then tilt the float up and scrape away as much excess grout as possible.

Wipe the grouted surface immediately with a damp sponge, making sure that the grout lines look the same. You may want to use the handle of a toothbrush or other rounded tool to scrape each joint. Rinse and wipe several times. Allow the grout to dry, then buff the surface to a shine with a dry cloth.

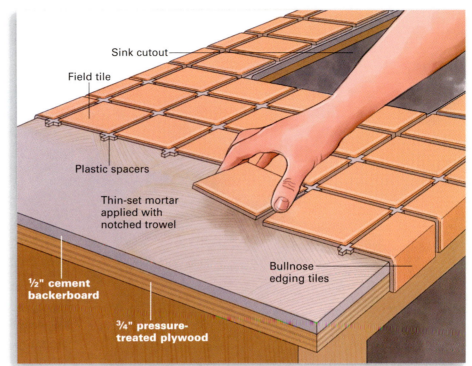

Sink cutout

Field tile

Plastic spacers

Thin-set mortar applied with notched trowel

Bullnose edging tiles

½" cement backerboard

¾" pressure-treated plywood

Position the tiles in a dry run—so you know exactly where each tile will go—before setting the tiles in thin-set.

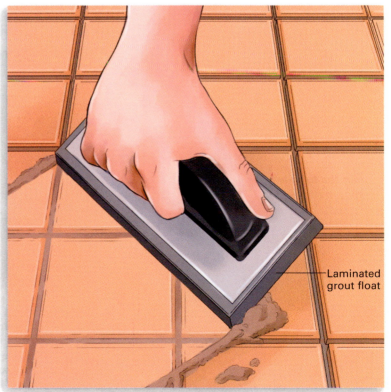

Laminated grout float

Press the grout into the joints with a grout float, then wipe it away. Sponge off the excess.

FOR THE BIRDS: FEEDERS AND HOUSES

Place a bird feeder where birds feel safe and where you can easily reach it for filling.

Observing birds can be exciting and relaxing. And they'll visit—or live in—your yard if you offer them something they need and may have trouble finding elsewhere—food and adequate shelter. A few simple structures will fill those needs.

LOCATING YOUR BIRD FEEDER

Experiment with different locations for the feeder until you find the one that works best. It should be close enough so you can easily observe the birds but far enough so they feel safe.

Purchase or make a feeder that is easy to open, and place it where you can easily refill it. To attract a variety of birds, install two feeders, one in a shady secluded spot and one out in the open.

BUILDING A HOPPER FEEDER

Use a knot-free 1×10 of redwood or cedar heartwood—a 4-foot piece is all you need for this project. Cut the pieces to the dimensions shown, apply sealer or stain to all the pieces, and let them dry. On the inside faces of both

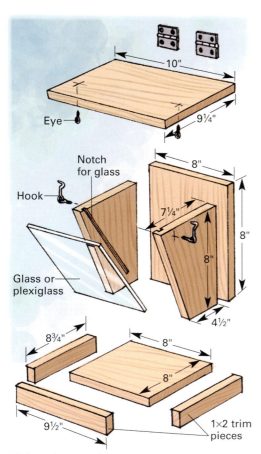

Make a hopper feeder out of 1× cedar or redwood that is knot-free, sanded, and treated.

SHISH KEBAB BIRD FEEDER

Birds eat almost anything and like variety in their diet. Here's an easy way to try out different foods to see which they like. Purchase a long barn spike and, with a hacksaw or cutting pliers, nip off the spike head at an angle to produce a point. Nail it a couple of inches into a tree or pole so it angles upward. Now treat your birds to any food that can be skewered.

side pieces, cut a groove with a circular saw that is ⅜ inch deep and wide enough for a piece of glass or acrylic to slide through easily. One cut should do it: A saw blade makes a cut ⅛ inch wide—just right for most pieces of glass or acrylic.

To assemble the pieces, drill pilot holes and drive 4d galvanized casing or box nails. Attach the back to the tray base, driving nails through the back and into the edge of the base. Attach the sides by nailing them to the back and the base. Then attach the trim around the tray base.

Set the lid on top of the feeder and mark the positions for the hinges and screws. Drill pilot holes and drive in small brass screws. To fasten the lid, mount hooks to the outside faces of the side pieces, and eyes to the edge of the top piece.

BIRDHOUSE SPECIFICATIONS

A birdhouse will attract different birds, depending on the size of the entrance hole you cut. Chickadees will enter if the hole is 1⅛ inches in diameter. A 1¼-inch hole will attract sparrows. Wrens, bluebirds, and some swallows will be attracted to a hole that is 1½ inches. To attract woodpeckers and finches, build a house with a floor size of 7 inches square and make the hole 2 inches in diameter.

Attach the house firmly to a tree or post that does not sway in the wind; birds like stability. Clean the bird house once a year with a mildewcide so the birds will return to nest.

EASY-OPEN BIRDHOUSE

Cut all the pieces to the dimensions shown and apply sealer or stain to each piece. Drill three or four ⅜-inch ventilation holes along the top edge of the sides and drainage holes in the bottom. Use a spade bit or hole saw to bore the entrance hole in the front piece.

Drill pilot holes and drive 4d galvanized casing or box nails to attach all the pieces.

Attach small cleats—¾-inch by ¾-inch and 4 inches long—to the inside face of the front piece to keep the face from cracking. On the back, front, and one side piece, measure and mark a line ½ inch from the bottom. Place the base just above the line, and attach.

Position the other side piece and mark screw positions for the hinges. Attach the hinges with small screws. Attach the hook-and-eye. Set the roof in position and nail through the top into the back, front, and the non-hinged side piece.

Check the preferences of birds common to your area. You may want to have several birdhouses in a variety of locations and with holes of different sizes to attract your favorite birds.

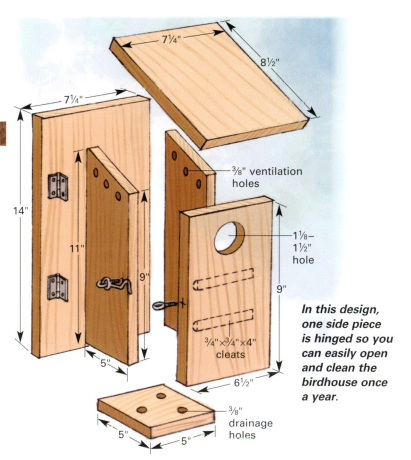

7¼"

8½"

⅜" ventilation holes

7¼"

14"

11"

9"

1⅛– 1½" hole

9"

5"

¾"×¾"×4" cleats

6½"

5"

5"

⅜" drainage holes

In this design, one side piece is hinged so you can easily open and clean the birdhouse once a year.

SANDBOX AND PLAY AREA

This structure packs much space to play into a small area. Wood chips and sand keep children safe if they fall off the tire swing, and a partially enclosed sandbox allows small children to play below while larger children enjoy more active play.

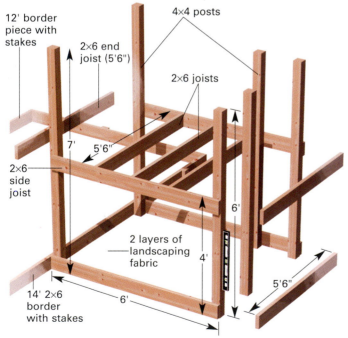

Install the posts taller than they need to be; you will cut them to height later. Make sure the 2×6 framing—with its top edge 4 feet above the ground—is level.

Stores offer plenty of ready-made playground sets; but if you're looking for the home-built variety, here's a versatile design. Children can find lots of ways to exercise their bodies and their imaginations in a sandbox, a tire swing, a climbing net, and a raised deck that can easily become a fort, a ship, or a playhouse.

Purchase the slide, net, ladder, and other equipment you may want to add, and modify the structure if necessary so all these elements will fit. (Make sure the openings for the slide and ladder are correct.)

Use wood that is rot-resistant and free of cracks and loose knots. No. 1–grade pressure-treated lumber and the heartwood of redwood are good choices. Sand surfaces periodically to keep children safe from splinters.

BUILD THE BASIC STRUCTURE

Choose a site that is fairly level so the sand will not spill out. Use a full sheet of plywood to mark the locations of the four corner postholes (see page 14 for other layout techniques). Dig the postholes at least 3 feet deep or as deep as local codes require, shovel in 4 inches of gravel, set the posts in the holes, and temporarily brace them so they are plumb on two adjacent sides (*see page 58*). Fill the holes with concrete and let it cure for three to seven days.

EXCAVATE: Dig away all the turf in the sandbox and wood-chip areas, tamp the soil firm, and lay down two layers of landscaping fabric. You may need to hold the fabric in place temporarily with rocks.

PLATFORM AND SIDE FRAMES: Attach all 2×6 framing pieces with three 3-inch deck screws at each intersection. Attach perimeter joists about 4 feet above ground level, as shown, making sure they are all level. Cut four evenly spaced inside joists and attach with joist hangers. Use 2×6s for the ground-level side frames. Attach them as shown, *opposite*, level and with the top edges at least 2 inches above the ground. In the wood-chip area below the swing, stake the framing with 2×4s every 4 or 5 feet.

CONSTRUCT THE PLATFORM AND RAILS: Cut and attach the decking boards. Then cut the posts at the heights shown. The two on the swing side are 4 feet above the deck; the other two are 3 feet above the deck. Install two more posts, one for an entryway at the top of the ladder and one for the slide. Attach the horizontal 2×6 rails as shown.

INSTALL THE PLAY EQUIPMENT

Build the framing for the tire swing and fill the area under the swing with wood chips. Fill the area under the decking with children's play sand. Both are available in bags, or they can be delivered loose by truck.

TIRE SWING: Choose a straight, uncracked 12-foot 4×6 for the swing beam. Drill a hole in its center and install an eyehook or a swivel hook designed for tire swings.

Build two A-frames with 2×6s as high as the top of the platform top rail, plus 30 inches. Notch the peaks (5½ inches deep by 3½ inches wide) in the center to hold the beam. Dig angled postholes, and set the beams in so the tops are even with the top of the top rail. Attach one frame to the side of the deck, and brace the other temporarily. Working with two helpers, set the beam in the notches. Miter both ends of the 2×4 supports at 45 degrees, and attach them to the beam and the top rail with screws.

LADDER, SLIDE, AND CLIMBING NET: Attach a manufactured ladder or build your own by anchoring three 2×4s below the ladder opening. Space them evenly for easy climbing. Follow manufacturer's instructions for anchoring the slide. If small children will use it, excavate and install a framed sandy area at the bottom of the slide. Attach the climbing net using the eyehooks and stakes provided by the manufacturer.

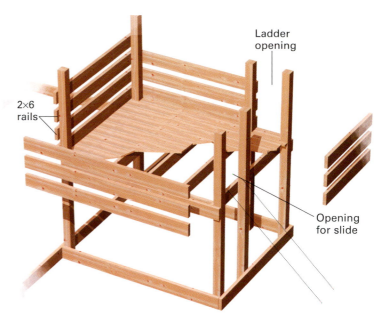

Ladder opening

2×6 rails

Opening for slide

Lay the decking out with consistent spacing; by adjusting the size of the spaces, you may be able to avoid rip-cutting the last piece. Attach the rails so all the spaces between them are the same.

Eyehooks

Stakes driven below surface

Make sure the net ladder you buy has eyehooks and stakes for attaching to the platform and to the ground. Drive the stakes deep—don't leave the tops exposed— so children can't pull them out or be injured.

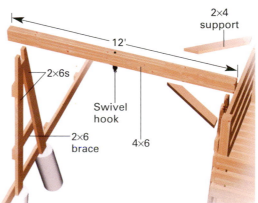

2×4 support

12'

2×6s

Swivel hook

2×6 brace

4×6

Build two A-frame braces, both to the height of the top rail. Purchase special tire-swing hardware, or affix a swivel hook in the center of the 4×6 beam and tie the rope to the tire.

GARDEN POND

Water gardens are inexpensive and relatively easy to install. A submersible pump will keep the water fresh and aerated so plants and fish will thrive. You can make a simple pond with a galvanized tub. Put in a recirculating pump and add plants.

This pond uses a rigid fiberglass preformed liner. They are available in a variety of sizes and shapes. A fiberglass liner costs more, it is stronger, and lasts longer.

EXCAVATE AND SET THE LINER

You can set a rigid liner completely in the ground, or place it on the ground and build a masonry or wood frame around it. The liner, *below*, is set partway in the ground, with the edges built up with stone. Dry set stone may shift slightly over time; for a more permanent installation, you can mortar the stones in place.

DIG THE HOLE: Call your utility companies to make sure you will not cut any electrical, gas, water, or phone lines. Then dig a hole deep enough for the pool to sit in, with its rim a foot above the ground. Place the liner in the hole to make sure it follows the contours of the hole. Remove rocks and dig out any roots larger than ½ inch in diameter. Check the bottom of the hole with a level, and tamp all the soil with a hand tamper or a piece of 4×4.

SCREED SAND: Spread about an inch of sand in the bottom, and use a short board to level it. Set the liner in, check it for level, and push down gently; the impressions it leaves will show you where you need to fill in with sand or scrape it away.

SET THE POND: It will take several attempts before the liner bottom sits flat on the sand. Once the bottom is firmly supported and the edges are level, run a hose to the pond and fill it with about 4 inches of water. Backfill the sides of the liner about up to the height of the water, tamp firm with a 2×4, then backfill again. Fill the pool with 4 more inches and repeat until the sides are filled.

INSTALL A WATER PUMP

Purchase a submersible pump powerful enough to aerate a pond of the size you have chosen. A magnetic-driven pump will use less

Scrape the sand smooth and flat with a short length of 2×4.

Working in 4-inch increments, alternately add water to the pond and backfill with tamped soil.

Stack stones to cover the sides of the pool. Backfill with sand or soil, and tamp lightly.

energy than a direct-driven pump; it will cost more but will save money to operate.

There are many kinds of fountainheads to choose from. Some bubble gently, some spray in mushroom shapes, and some shoot water out of a decorative ornament.

Installing the pump is easy: Place it on a concrete pad or other stable surface, and adjust the head to the height you desire. Then plug it into a GFCI (ground fault circuit interrupter) receptacle.

BUILD STONE SIDING

Natural stone usually looks best around water, but you also can use concrete pavers or interlocking retaining wall blocks.

Dig away the turf around the pond wherever the stones will be laid. Using a flat spade, slice the trench so that grass will grow right up to the stones. Tamp the soil firm with a hand tamper or a piece of 4×4.

Lay the bottom course several inches away from the liner so the upper courses can be battered back (see pages 62-63). Check each stone for stability and scrape away or add soil as needed so it doesn't wobble. Backfill the area between the stones and the liner with a mixture of firmly tamped sand and soil.

Lay the succeeding courses set back about ½ inch. Backfill after laying each course. When you reach the top course, use wider stones to cover the liner edge. For extra strength, set this top course in mortar.

ADD PLANTS

You may want to cover at least part of the bottom with smooth pebbles or rocks. Most municipal water contains chlorine, which can harm water animals and plants. After filling the pool, add a dechlorinator before adding fish or plants. When topping off evaporated pond water, run the hose very slowly.

CHOOSE PLANTS:

Purchase plants in containers that you can set on the bottom of the pool. Consult with your supplier for the plants that work best in your area and are suited to the conditions in your pool.

■ **SUBMERGED PLANTS** add a bit of oxygen to the water and absorb carbon dioxide and minerals, which inhibit algae growth. They help filter the water and can provide cover for fish. Plant a pot about every 3 square feet. Milfoil and hornwort are two good choices.

■ **FLOATERS** have leaves and flowers on top, and their roots dangle in the water. Set them in the water, without a pot. Don't let them cover more than half of the water surface or they could harm the water.

■ **DEEP-WATER PLANTS,** such as water lilies, need their pots to be set deep in the water.

■ **MARGINALS** grow in shallow water; place their pots on the shelf near the edge of the pond. They add color and interest and help make a visual transition from pool to yard.

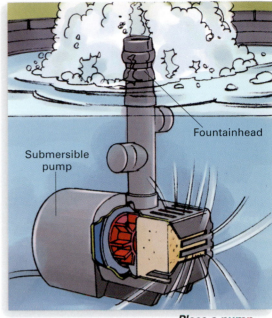

Fountainhead

Submersible pump

Place a pump so it bubbles or sprays upward, oxygenating the water and providing pleasure to eyes and ears.

Use a variety of plants to add oxygen, provide cover for fish, and make your pond a captivating water garden.

GLOSSARY

AGGREGATE: Gravel or crushed rock; mixed with sand, portland cement, and water to form concrete.

BACKFILL: Soil used to fill in an excavation.

BASE: A prepared surface of gravel or sand that will support bricks, pavers, or concrete.

BATTER BOARD: A board frame supported by stakes set back from the corners of a structure.

BRICK GRADE: A brick's durability rating, such as severe weather (SW).

BRICKSET: A wide-bladed chisel used for cutting bricks and concrete blocks.

BUTT JOINT: A joint of two pieces fastened end to end, end to face, or end to edge.

BUTTER: To apply mortar on bricks or blocks with a trowel before laying them.

CEMENT: A powder that serves as the binding element in concrete and mortar.

COMMON BRICK: General-purpose brick, can be used for patio paving in milder climates.

CONCRETE: Building material made by mixing water with sand, gravel, and cement.

CONTROL JOINT: A groove tooled into a concrete slab during finishing to prevent uncontrolled cracking later on.

COURSE: A row of masonry units, such as bricks or stones.

CUBES OR BANDS: Pre-grouped quantities of pavers that will cover 16 lineal feet.

DARBY: A long-bladed float used to smooth large surfaces of freshly poured concrete.

DRY-STACKED WALL: A wall of stones laid without mortar.

DRY WELL: A hole at a level below the patio site, connected to the site by a drainpipe.

EDGER: A tool for rounding and smoothing concrete edges to finish and strengthen them.

EDGING: A border used to contain and define a surface; common materials are brick, concrete, plastic, and wood.

EXPOSED AGGREGATE: A concrete finish characterized by small stones imbedded in the surface.

FINISHING: The final smoothing stage in concrete work.

FLAGSTONE: Flat stone in irregular shapes; the most common are granite, bluestone, redstone, sandstone, limestone, and slate.

FLOAT: A wood or metal hand tool used to smooth and compress wet concrete.

FLUSH: On the same plane, or level with, the surrounding surface.

FOOTING: A small foundation, usually made of concrete, used to support a post.

FROST HEAVE: An upward movement of soil caused when moist soil freezes.

FROST LINE: The maximum depth frost normally penetrates the soil.

GROUT: A thin mortar mixture used to fill the joints between tiles.

HAND DRILL: A small sledge hammer; used for breaking flagstones and driving larger chisels, such as bricksets.

JOINTER: A tool used for making control joints, or grooves, in concrete surfaces to control cracking.

LANDSCAPE FABRIC: Tightly woven fabric that allows water to flow through, but prevents weeds from growing up.

LAP JOINT: The joint formed when one member overlaps another.

LEVEL: The condition that exists when any type of surface is at true horizontal.

MASONRY CEMENT: Portland cement and hydrated lime mixed for preparing mortar.

MASON'S HAMMER: A tempered-steel hammer with a square face and a chisel-shaped claw.

MITER JOINT: The joint formed between two beveled edges.

MORTAR: A mixture of masonry cement, masonry sand, and water.

NOMINAL DIMENSIONS: The actual dimensions of a masonry unit, plus the thickness of the mortar joints on one end and at the top or bottom.

PAVERS: Cast concrete blocks, often dyed and shaped to fit in interlocking patterns.

PAVING BRICK: Brick of very dense clay, fired to high temperatures to be hard and durable.

PLAN DRAWING: An overhead view of a structure, which shows locations of footings and framing.

PLUMB: True vertical.

PREMIX: Packaged mixtures of ingredients used for preparing concrete or mortar.

PRESSURE-TREATED: Lumber or plywood soaked in solutions to make the wood resistant to water.

READY-MIX: Concrete that is mixed in a truck on its way to the job site.

REBAR (REINFORCING ROD): Steel rod used to reinforce concrete and masonry structures.

REINFORCING WIRE MESH: Steel screen used to reinforce concrete.

RETAINING WALL: A wall constructed to hold soil in place.

RIVER ROCK: Medium-sized stones smoothed by river or lake water.

RUBBLE: Uncut stone, often used for dry-stacked walls.

SCRATCH COAT: The first coat of mortar or plaster, roughened (scratched) so the next coat will stick to it.

SCREED: A straight edge used to level concrete as it is poured into a form or to level a sand base.

SET: The process during which mortar or concrete hardens.

SETBACK: The minimum distance between a property line and a structure, set by local codes.

SITE PLAN: A map showing the location of a new building project on a piece of property.

SPACER BLOCKS: Small blocks, also called dobie blocks, used to support reinforcing wire mesh for pouring concrete.

SQUARE: A 90-degree corner.

STRIKING: The process of finishing a mortar joint.

SUB-BASE: Compacted soil or gravel beneath a base surface of gravel or sand.

TAMPER: A tool for compacting soil, sand, or other loose materials.

TROWEL: A flat and oblong or pointed tool used for handling or finishing concrete and mortar.

WATER LEVEL: A tool for establishing level over long distances or irregular surfaces.

YARD: A unit of volume by which ready-mix concrete is sold; equal to a square yard (27 cubic feet).

METRIC CONVERSIONS

U.S. Units to Metric Equivalents			Metric Units to U.S. Equivalents		
To Convert From	Multiply By	To Get	To Convert From	Multiply By	To Get
Inches	25.4	Millimeters	Millimeters	0.0394	Inches
Inches	2.54	Centimeters	Centimeters	0.3937	Inches
Feet	30.48	Centimeters	Centimeters	0.0328	Feet
Feet	0.3048	Meters	Meters	3.2808	Feet
Yards	0.9144	Meters	Meters	1.0936	Yards
Square inches	6.4516	Square centimeters	Square centimeters	0.1550	Square inches
Square feet	0.0929	Square meters	Square meters	10.764	Square feet
Square yards	0.8361	Square meters	Square meters	1.1960	Square yards
Acres	0.4047	Hectares	Hectares	2.4711	Acres
Cubic inches	16.387	Cubic centimeters	Cubic centimeters	0.0610	Cubic inches
Cubic feet	0.0283	Cubic meters	Cubic meters	35.315	Cubic feet
Cubic feet	28.316	Liters	Liters	0.0353	Cubic feet
Cubic yards	0.7646	Cubic meters	Cubic meters	1.308	Cubic yards
Cubic yards	764.55	Liters	Liters	0.0013	Cubic yards

To convert from degrees Fahrenheit (F) to degrees Celsius (C), first subtract 32, then multiply by $\frac{5}{9}$.

To convert from degrees Celsius to degrees Fahrenheit, multiply by $\frac{9}{5}$, then add 32.